Don't Tell Me It's Too Late
Revised Edition
By
Donald L. Alford

ADLAM Publishers

4300 Commerce Ct. #300-7

Lise, IL 60532

www.apostledonaldalford.com

630.779.3188

Unless otherwise noted, all scripture quotations are from the King James Version

Revised Edition (ADLAM Publishers) 4/2011

ISBN: ISBN-10 0983576602

ISBN-13 9780983576600

Printed in the United States of America

Copresco

Carol Stream, IL

DEDICATIONS

To My Father the late Dr. James B. Alford and to my Mother Minnie M. Alford. To my lovely wife, Pastor Gloria Alford, who God sent to me over 30 years ago to be my companion, friend and lover. She has been a constant encourager. I call her Babe. (We've called each other that endearing name for as long as we've been together) Babe, you have been there for me through the thick and the thin. I love you and really appreciate God for giving you to me. It would have been extremely difficult to make it thus far without you being by my side. Hey, Babe thanks for singing alto on this project as well. I want to dedicate this book to all my children: my oldest son, Donald L. Alford II, thanks for helping your dad as Producer with this recording, you are a blessing. To my daughter-in-law, Rasheeda Alford, thanks for supporting your husband and our son, to G-Daddy's babies: Dajia, Donald III, and DeVaughn. I dedicate this book to my middle son, Stephon J. Alford, who has had to listen and help give sound business advice to assist me through this process moreover, who also sang on this project. To my special son, Terrell M. Alford who I love, he is God's gift to my wife and I. To Maggie and Chris who has been there for us all the way. I dedicate this book to my only daughter Ms. Brianna Lanae Nicole Alford who sang on this project; thanks for your support and I am proud of you for your academic accomplishments, keep up the good work.

To my brother Perry J. Alford Sr. and wife, Erna who have been strong supporters and who have spoken prophetic words often to encourage me and push me towards destiny. To my oldest brother I love him and pray all God's goodness upon his life James B. Alford Jr. and his wife, Carolyn. To my sister the late Beatrice Alford Clency, you taught me so much.

I dedicate this book to Stella Windom, what can I say, you've been there like no other when others were not around you were there to hear my cry and speak words of comfort down through the years. PJ Alford Jr. his wife Carmen, Mi'kylah & Perry (little P), Minister Mike & Alita Abron, Sean Alford, Keisha Sally, who has worked fervently on this project, her daughter Taneisha Caldwell, Sonia and JB Alford, Brittnee, Jeniece & James.

To the late Pastor Alfred Windom Sr. I dedicate this book. He encouraged me every time he saw me. He believed in me and told me I could do whatever God said. To Mother Georgia Windom, who has been nothing but a strong supporter down through the years! Pastor Alfred & Octavia Windom, André, Ashur, Asim, Bailey & Alexis, Elder Nathaniel Windom, Kristin, Jeremy & Caleb, Tim Windom and Joe Windom; thank you for being so supportive. To our son, David Dickerson, thanks for all you do.

To my extended family for many years, my sister Elder Ronia Bosley, you have been in my life since childhood. Thanks for your love and support down through the years.

What a wonderful encourager you are to me. Thanks Ronia!

To my sister Elder Jean Grace, thank you for being one of my closest friends ever and sister for over 40 years. We have wept together, prayed together and laughed together. No matter what you have been right there for me and I'll never forget. My other son, Pastor De Andre Patterson, who stood with me through it all for over 20 years assisting me as Minister of Music and Assistant Pastor, thank you son, for your support and dedication, you will never be forgotten by your dad. To my daughter, Pat Patterson, Big Daddy's boy, Dylan Patterson, I honor you with this dedication. To my friend and brother Pastor Willie O. Dukes, one that I could always depend on no matter what, he was there for me; I will not ever forget you. Thanks for being there for me through it all. To your very supportive wife Linda, and to the entire Dukes Family. We Love You! I want to dedicate this book to the late Deacon Ruben Locke, former President of Holy Spirit Records, who had a dream and saw me taking this anointing around the world. He saw greatness upon my life and invested in me. I will never forget you Ruben, and to his wife Shirley Locke, son & daughter, John & Jackie. Thanks for your support. Your kindness will never be forgotten. I dedicate this book to the late Mel Collins, President of Glory Records who believed in me like no other individual ever had. He helped launch my first album in 1979. He was the first one to invest in my music ministry by funding the project after it sat in the studio on a shelf for over a year. Thanks Mel Collins, I am glad to have known someone with a heart like that. Thanks Dorothy Holiday for your support to Mel Collins and to our family.

To my Progressive Family, I love and appreciate you for allowing me to serve as your Senior Pastor. I especially want to dedicate this book to my Associate Pastors, Elders, Ministers, Deacons, Directors, Ministry Leaders, Board of Directors, Executive Staff, Finance Committee, Deacons, Staff Assistants, and Laity.

To Elder Corina Thomas who served as my Administrative Assistant for over 18 years. You were instrumental in bringing us to the next level. Minister Karen Jackson, thank you for stepping in during a time when I needed much help in the area of Special Events. I dedicate this book to an elite group of women: Elder Jean Grace, Elder Martha Michels, Pastor Hazel Douglas and Pastor Evelyn Crawford, who served faithfully as specially assigned intercessors for me.

When I first began as Pastor and to date, they are yet positioned in prayer for the ministry and me. These women stood the storms that came upon the ministry and yet remain steadfast and unmovable. I love you all so much and will never forget your labor of love in God's vineyard down through the years. I want to dedicate this book to Minister Wanda Sharp. Words cannot express my gratitude for the kindness that you have expressed toward my wife, my family and me for many years. I will never forget you, because what you always wanted was to see the best come into our lives, we are grateful for your love, care and concern for our family. I dedicate this book to another one of my sons, Minister Darnell Wallace, your wife Tata and children, because you were there for me to help lift my head when others did not know, thank you so much for believing in your dad. Thanks for keeping me looking great, groomed and young by the head. Darrell & Tiffany Brown, you helped me look great too! I especially want to dedicate this book to one I admire, Pastor Carl Smith. He is another one of my sons who saw the best in me and I saw the best in him. Together we have encouraged each other, spoke into each other's lives through the most difficult seasons in our lives. However, I have hit the vain of a turnaround in my life. Thanks for believing that the rest of my days will be the best of my days, both naturally and spiritually. To our Ministry Operations Manager, Elder Cornelius Williams and my Administrative Assistant, Elder Adrienne White, I really appreciate you for both stepping in and taking up the helm to help regain strength to the administration arm of the church. What a blessing you both are to the ministry, my wife and I. Elder Floyd Wilkinson, thanks for the season you gave of yourself to support and assist me in ministry. Elder Al Cleveland, Lady Lori and family, thanks Al for believing in me and being my personal organist for many years.

To Elaine Meaux, for many years of dedicated service. Thanks for hanging in there with us through the ups and downs. To Denise Hendry for many years of dedicated service. Thanks Lorraine Duvalier, for your contribution to the ministry, as well.

To the Progressive Fellowship For Kingdom Builders (PFFKB) Family: Apostle Eric & Pastor Lisa Harris, Pastor W. Charles Morrow, Pastor Edward Jenkins, Pastor Ricky & Lady Elaine Harris, Pastors Victor and Gayla Walker, Pastors Otis & Shonda Burns, Apostle Jonathan Swain, Apostle Derrick White, Pastors Dwayne and Beverly Jordan. (Albuquerque, NM), Apostle C.D & Prophetess Nell Dixon (Houston, TX)
Ministry Gifts: Pastor Dollie Sherman, Evangelist Brenda Finley & Prophet/Elder Cornelius & Minister Chinata Williams. To All Future PFFKB Family Members.

ACKNOWLEDGEMENTS/ADDITIONAL DEDICATIONS:

This list of the people has been a tremendous blessing in my life. Some are Generals in the body of Christ and who have made significant deposits into my life and ministry, I personally appreciate all of our family members as well:

The Late Mother EM Vann

Percy Bady	Allan Hunter
Pastor Darius & Deborah Brooks	Elder Joel & Aline Fields
Mother Virda Love/Family	Sister Earline Hale
Donald & Sharmaine Webb	Maggie Foggie

Deacon Robert & Geneva Williams

Deacon Clarence & Alpha Jones

Pastor W.J. & Lady Lori Campbell

Deacon Steve & Amber Grace

Deacon Kendall Faber

Elder Etrenda Faber

Elder & Sister Jeffrey Spence

Sister Isabelle Wright

Sister Denise Hendry

Deacon Robert Porter

Elder Randy Gordan

Rev. Foster

Dr. Charles Clency

Pastors Dwayne & Beverly Jordan

Elder Deverrick Crawford

Mother Emily Boulware-Foster

The Late Mother June Hillery

The Late Annie B. Bosley

Mother Fannie Nuness

The Late Sis. Vera Grace

The Late Elder Wilmon Grace

The Late Elder Ernest Grace

The Late Elder Hillery

The Late Missionary Felvia Hale

The Late Evang. Dorothy Ervin

The Late Elder Jacquelyn Hendry

Bishop & Mother Willie Chambliss

The Late Missionary M.L. Parham

Christopher Foggie

The Staff of P.A.E.C.

The Late James A. Windom

To All of Our Godchildren

God Daughter Shonna Edwards

God Son Jon Gordan

God Son Jeremy Williams

God Daughter Rachel Maselli

Aunt Dorothy Shelton

Rev. Dr. Marvin McMickle

Mrs. Peggy McMickle

Cousin Paul James McMickle

Cousin Sonya Muhammad

Bishop W.H. Bonner

Apostle R.D. Henton

Deborah Mines

Mazie Robinson

Katrina Taylor

Tamie Crawford

Mr. Lee Johnson

Pastor Dorothy Blaylark

Samuel Brown

Les Brown

Apostle Janice Agnew

Bishop Jerome Scott

Brenda Smith

Diane Brown

James & Ruby Chatham

Vanessa & Sherman Baker

Pastor Kenneth Hollingsworth

Brenda & Leroy Edwards

Dr. Mildred Harris

Pastor Tracy DeVolt

Rev. Marshall

Deacon Lauderdale & Michelle Massey

The Late Prophetess Rosemary Maselli

The Late Aunt Marthetta G. McMickle
(My Dad, Papa's sister)

The Late Evang. Elnora Rodgers

Pastor James & Regina Williams

Apostle Gerald Griffith

Pastor John White

Apostle Walter & Lady Delores Bates

Bishop Darrell & Pastor Pamela Hines

Queenie Lenox & Family

Laverne Gregory & Family

Apostle Rodney & Pastor Joyce Dennis

Jewell Partee & Family

Minnie Wilson & Family

Gary Lacey, Outback Steakhouse, Wheaton, IL

Thanks for the wonderful food and blue bell ice cream!

SPECIAL THANKS:

Douglas Miller

David Dickerson

Julia Jackson

Crystal Lewis Turner

Asaleana Crawford

Elder Cornelius Williams

Pastor Gloria Alford

Stephon J. Alford

Donald L. Alford II

Brianna L.N. Alford

Estella "Stell" Windom

EDITOR

Dr. Sharon Kissane

First Edition

Special Acknowledgements to:

Bishop I.V. Hilliard & Pastor Bridget Hilliard,

Our Spiritual Covering & the AIM Family

We appreciate your leadership and dedication to

the Kingdom!

A Very Special Thanks To The Editing Team of This Revised Edition

Minister Rosalind Banks

Loura Banks-Whitney

Mrs. Cellie Banks

Rev. Dr. Ronald Beauchamp, Director,
Niebuhr Center - Elmhurst College

Evan Cunningham
(Junior, Business major – Detroit,MI)

Aspyn Jones
(Freshman, Journalism major – Chicago, IL

A heartfelt thanks to Lynn Buck, Jessica Pinkous and Steve Johnson at Copresco, Carol Stream, IL. The staff is incredible!!! Lynn, you're the best! We really appreciate all of your expertise and deligience! You and the staff really aim to please.

Thank you Kjellberg Printing, Wheaton, IL for the First Edition contribution, Cheryl, Gary and Kevin, thanks for the geniune assistance with the printing of the dust jackets, bookmarks, etc.

I was a wakened early in the morning on Thursday, July 29th to a message at around 3 am I know that came from God to write my first book. This book is for those persons who have had some disappointing, horrific experiences in life and feel like it's too late to achieve and see their vision or dreams become a reality. Has every phase of your life left you even more devastated? As I read the scriptures, it's stated that man is born of a few days and full of trouble. Be assured that no one is getting by from having trouble somewhere at some time. Therefore, you must simply make up your mind, face the situation and say, "Yes, I've been affected by what has happened in my life." Don't be afraid to admit that you've wasted a whole lot of time crying over your past. You've got to get an "I don't care" attitude against every voice that speaks to you. Speak positive words every chance you get the opportunity to do so. The power of life and death are in your mouth…Speak into your own future! You must rise up and face your regrets and possibly missed opportunities in life. Stand, up and say to the devil, "Don't Tell Me It's Too Late!" Do what God has ordained and purposed for your life and start living.

TABLE OF CONTENTS

I. THE MANDATE

II. THE METHOD OF DEVELOPMENT

III. THE MODEL OF MERCY

IV. THE MIRACLE THROUGH OBEDIENCE

I. THE MANDATE

CHAPTER 1

GOD HAS A PURPOSE FOR YOUR LIFE

Jeremiah 1:5; Romans 8:28-30; John 18:36-37

THE DIFFICULTY IN UNCOVERING PURPOSE

The saddest thing in life is knowing that some people live life and then die never realizing their purposes. Can you imagine how many days, months and years are consumed with various ideas, thoughts and imaginations that run through our heads? There are brilliant concepts and/or business plans with tremendous creativity, but none of those dreams come to pass.

In many cases, we pursue things by what others say and allow them to determine our purposes. Unconsciously, we expect them to guide our lives. What directions should we take? Who should be our friends, our associates and even our companions? Then, if we don't like who they pick for us to befriend, they become upset and consequently, we become uncomfortable. Without knowing it, we have become people pleasers. This is extremely dangerous and deadly because you are now allowing yourself to become dependent upon the views and opinions of others. This is crippling and a very unhealthy condition.

I pray that you find God for yourself and develop a relationship with Him. This is so you can get to know Him in a real and intimate way. After that, you can begin to accept and love who you are. You will begin to know that

He had purpose for creating you and it won't matter what others think or say about you.

It's hard to accept that you've been deceived all this time and you have wasted time permitting people to pull you here and there. After giving you suggestions and ideas, you'll come to find out that they didn't do anything but confuse you even more.

The search for the truth of your existence can be frustrating. If you seek God to find the truth about who you are and what He's called you to do in life, you will find it. However, you must be willing to spend valuable time in prayer and in God's word to find truth. Through prayer, we find out the heart of God and His desires for our lives. Seek and ye shall find (Matthew 7:7)!

Prayer is the most powerful force on earth. It's through prayer that we communicate with the creator, our Father. The purpose of all this is to go through the "peeling off process." That is, the process of allowing God to remove out of your life the mental misconceptions concerning yourself. I guarantee that you'll find the things you believed about yourself, based upon what was spoken to you, are not true.

The dilemma is being apprehended by God and trying to apprehend Him. The Apostle Paul had a difficult time dealing with the fact that he was chosen by the grace and power of God. God's love for him was shown and portrayed to him by saving him, delivering him and calling him to be an Apostle to the Gentiles. Paul gradually began to appreciate and to see God's goodness in the fact that He laid His hand on him.

While he was yet in his sin, he was loved by God and summoned by God to preach the gospel of Jesus Christ. In other words, Paul was saying he knew that God had taken a hold of his life, his mind and his spirit. It is within everyone's ability to walk in fellowship with God and please Him. However, when one desires to do good, evil is ever present (Romans 7:21). Paul had a rough time walking in the divine grace of God, into which we are accepted not because of our good works, but by the grace of God.

Let this be a lesson: Don't try within your human efforts to fulfill a spiritual commandment through natural and religious rituals. This can never happen. To do so will only leave you frustrated and disappointed.

EXPERIENCE THE PURSUIT

I went through the same dilemma even though I had a heart and love for God and His people. Searching as a Pastor's son, I was very open in my attempts to find God in a deep intimate way for myself. However, due to my openness and sincere desire to please him, there were those who I allowed to speak into my life. They brought tremendous confusion concerning my destiny. I didn't want to do anything that would not please God, so I became very vulnerable. I thank God for His mercy and His grace, as I began to learn the voice of the Lord for myself by developing a close relationship with Him.

He spoke to me at the water fountain on the 1st floor of our church in October 1975 while I was about to drink. The voice of the Lord said to me, "I've anointed you to preach the gospel!" I rose up and looked at Pastor James Williams, who was one of the ministers under my Dad, Dr. James Benjamin Alford, Sr. at that time. Then he spoke out to confirm my calling by saying, "Did God just call you to preach?" and I said to him in awe, "Yes!" It was as though he was tuned into the conversation between the Lord and I. I was amazed and shocked at the same time. I then entered a growth stage to learn about what God called me to do. I thank God for not letting me aimlessly try to discover the path I should take.

THE CHOSEN VESSELS IN THE BIBLE

There were numerous people assigned to great tasks, who had tremendous insufficiencies. God chooses to use those who normally feel as though they just can't do what He wants them to do. I believe they represent the voice of millions that say, "Lord I want to please you, but I just can't do what you want me to do." I can understand why some wish they could bargain and negotiate with God to get Him to change His mind. Nevertheless, when He thought of you,

He had already predetermined what you were designed and assigned to do in your life.

Moses' deficiency was speaking with a stutter. Therefore, he could not perceive how he could go and speak on behalf of Jehovah, and to face Pharaoh to tell him that God said, "Let my people go."

Gideon wondered how God could choose him. Gideon's family was poor and he said he was the least in his father's household. Nevertheless, the Angel of the Lord came to him and the first thing he said to Gideon was, "...The Lord is with thee, thou mighty man of valour" (Judges 6:12). That declaration sanctioned that God had chosen or preordained Gideon. Could it be that this is exactly what's going on concerning you?

I believe with all my heart that He does not call us to try to begin a relationship or a conversation with us. He is not trying to find out what He wants to do with our lives. Rather, when He calls us, He already knows what He wants to do in and through our lives. In addition, He knows we are already qualified and graced to do what He calls us to do. He knows that we have the ability, the make-up and the character given through Christ Jesus, who enables us to accomplish tasks. God needs us to understand what He already knows about us. We are preordained, called and fully equipped to complete our assigned tasks even if we don't feel like we are qualified.

Jeremiah said, "I'm too young; I am a child and they definitely won't listen to me" (Jeremiah Chapter 1). But, God doesn't have a problem with whom He decides to use. This is a lesson that God is teaching the church as a whole and each of us individually. Being chosen is not based upon whether you feel qualified or not, and it's not based upon your acceptance of God's choice. If you're the one, old enough or not, then you're the one!

Sometimes, people end up doing what God calls them to do regardless of the challenges they may encounter. Some people die refusing to do what God called them to do. Jeremiah's task wasn't a favorable one, because he had to speak out against unrighteousness amongst God's chosen, the nation of Israel. Moses and Gideon both had challenges. Through Moses' leadership, the children of Israel came out of bondage after four hundred thirty (430) years of captivity (Exodus Chapter 12). After being fully persuaded and convinced, Gideon stood tall and defeated the Midianites with only three hundred (300) men. Gideon had to face thousands of Midianites with God's chosen number of three hundred (300) to show not only the Israelites, but also himself that when God chooses you, you don't need what others typically depend on (Judges Chapter 7). There's a certain grace that's released upon those called to do specific assignments and it's dangerous to try to operate in an office that you're not graced or chosen to serve in.

Sometime chosen people are placed in awkward and embarrassing situations. For example, Mary, the mother of Jesus, was chosen to carry the Christ child, but she had to deal with shame and blame of doing so. Since she was engaged to be married, this was quite an unusual situation. How do you explain to family and friends that you and Joseph were not sleeping together and you were not sleeping around? Mary carried the burden of knowing that her assignment would cast doubt and questions about her future marriage. But, scripture states that Mary was given the assignment because she was "Highly favored among women" (Luke 1:28). Can you imagine the task and the awesome responsibility? Mary had to do what no other woman on this earth has done or will ever do.

Elizabeth was pregnant in her old age; how do you think she explained that? She had to deal with the gossip, the comments and the facial expressions. Possibly, people were saying she was too old for something like that to happen. Elizabeth knew it had to be God, after all of those years of waiting and nothing happening until then. Some probably said, "I don't know if Zechariah could get her pregnant, maybe that's someone else's child." All kinds of accusations could have come from that situation. God had a plan even in that. God had to shut the mouth of Zechariah until the child was born (Luke 1:11-22).

GOD'S METHOD OF SELECTION

God always chooses people who try to justify why they should not be the ones that He should have chosen. I say that God is a glory seeker. He seeks out ways which allow Him to receive credit for His plans. He loves to choose people who have issues and don't match up to the status quo. He loves to select those who others frown upon and say nasty things about. He seems to find pleasure in picking people whom others feel are insignificant. He loves to clean up messy lives. He empowers and raises them up to use them in His service. Some respond and say, "How could that be or why did God choose him or her?" This is what I love about God; He doesn't need anyone else's approval.

One of the major purposes of the church and the Pastor of the local church is to help assist, direct and/or prepare individuals for what God has called them to do. The Senior Pastor is not to prevent individuals from doing what God called them to do. He or she should use the wisdom received from God to guide individuals. An individual's perception of his or her Pastor determines his or her ability to accept or reject spiritual instruction.

Be open to spiritual instructions and directions from your Pastor. A true shepherd, one after God's own heart, will never hold you back or intentionally hurt you. A true shepherd will do all he or she can to protect you from wolves in sheep's clothing, and from yourself.

Make sure that you are under good leadership, because your destiny itself is at stake. You're fighting enough, just dealing with the fact that God chose you and perhaps you're having a difficult time trying to embrace it fully. Always remember, there must be a reason why your fight is so great; it's because your assignment is so great. Your assignment will cause havoc to the kingdom of darkness, but glory to the kingdom of God. Remember you are God's chosen!

God, in many cases, will choose those who struggle with esteem issues or other deficiencies that they fight with on a daily bases within themselves. Satan's job is to keep your weaknesses and regrets in the forefront of your mind. I call it "mental baggage." If the devil can keep you focused on what you can't do, then he has succeeded. There is so much garbage that we've unintentionally collected down through the years that has affected us. There were words, conversations, opinions, views and thoughts that are not biblically based, but man based. Many of those words came from people who had various sad experiences that they brought upon themselves. These are sad people. They were never renewed in their thinking through the word of God, and they began spreading their experiences to others who sought knowledge. As a result of seeking knowledge, individuals were more emotionally damaged then they were before seeking knowledge.

If a person appears older or seems to have wisdom, listen to what he or she says before taking his or her words as law. If he or she doesn't speak words of wisdom based upon what God says about that subject, don't accept it. It's sad that generations are infected by the ignorance of individuals who have lived lives without the knowledge of God's word.

Let this be another important lesson: Make sure that you are receiving guidance from a healthy and solid biblically based environment, because it could spell life or death for you. Are you laying your head down in a person's lap who has a spirit like the one Delilah had? When Sampson lay in Delilah's lap, she whispered "sweet nothings" to him as she cut off his strength, his hair. Some "Delilah" spirits seek individuals with self-esteem issues and lure them into cults and various strong and controlling environments. Remember: Not everybody is for you. Some people want to diminish the strength that you have, they "seek to cut your hair off."

You have to know who you are. If you don't know yourself, others will tell you who are you and what you can or cannot achieve in life. God never intended for another man or woman to identify who you are.

You cannot allow your pain or lack of self-motivation to make you become dependent on another's eyes to lead you. God wants you to seek Him, and He will show you your worth to Him.

You will then become confident in His choice, which is "You," and fulfilling your calling. God knew you before you were born. God is not shocked over who you are or what He called you to do. There is nothing that you have done or will do that God doesn't know about. He's alpha and omega, the beginning and the end; the first and the last. God is the one who ordained and orchestrated specific situations within our individual lives. Therefore, the steps of a good man are ordered by the Lord and He delights in his way.

You were not chosen because you were going to represent God as the perfect "Lamb of God." No, Jesus is that perfect Lamb of God. That's why he came. He died and arose for us, to save us from our sins. He took the blame of our shame, so we could be accepted into the family of God and be used by God for His glory.

God already knew that you would see yourself unqualified and incapable of doing the tasks given because of your struggles and perceived inabilities. Yet, you are God's chosen. Wow! What a privilege to be who God wanted, even if you're not who man wants! God doesn't make mistakes; therefore, you are not a mistake. "You" were born for a purpose. Sometimes the most difficult thing in life is to accept that you are not a mistake and that you were not just born, but you were born for a cause; a reason; an ordained purpose. God brought you here specifically to fulfill an assignment and your assignment has been given to you and to you alone. Only you can fulfill this responsibility. You are to reach out and touch specific people and give those people Jesus Christ through your life style, your message and your love.

Jesus came into the world for a cause. He knew that he would become a sacrifice and die on the cross for our sins. He was buried and arose from the dead with all power in his hands. Jesus knew that if he didn't complete his mission, that you and I would not have the opportunity to receive eternal life and we all would be lost forever, eternally.

But thanks be unto God who gives us the victory through Jesus Christ, our Lord (1 Corinthians 15:57). So, get prepared for an exciting future doing the will of God. If you could only see what God has in store for you, you would literally be blown away. According to 1 Corinthians 2:9 and Romans 8:28, "Eye hath not seen, nor ear heard, the things which God has in store for them that love Him and for them who are the called according to His purpose." When you grow tired of doing what God has called you to do, think about Galatians 6:9, "Be not weary in well doing, for in due season ye shall reap if you faint not."

You can no longer allow your present circumstances to "pro-phe-lie" to you and tell you that nothing good is in the future for you. You must have faith and get a glimpse of the hope for a bright future, just as God gave Caleb and

Joshua. God showed Joshua and Caleb the Promised Land, but they could not live there because it was not their time. This is where we often mess up: We can seek or desire to become successful in life, but achieving success is another ball game.

Job 14:1 says, "Man that is born of a woman is of a few days but full of trouble." This is an unpleasant fact that the Apostle Paul affirms in his letter to the church of Corinth, "We are troubled on every side..." (2 Corinthians 4:8). There is no way around trouble. You must face it and endure it, and you'll get through it with the help of God through Jesus Christ. Since you can't get around trouble, begin living with expectation and great anticipation. Wake up every day, saying, "This is the day that the Lord hath made. I will rejoice and be glad in it!" Have an attitude where you choose to have joy and to be at peace with life, no matter what life may bring. Be at peace because Jesus is with you in every storm. You're at peace because Jesus not only sends his presence around you, but it dwells in you. Jesus told his disciples in Matthew 28:20, "Lo, I am with you always, even until the end of the world." The fact that Jesus is always with you means that Philippians 4:13 is much more encouraging, "(You) can do all things through Christ which strengthens (you)." Not only is Jesus with you, but he is also more than you are going through. 1 John 4:4 says that, "Greater is he that's in (you) than he that is in the world.

THE SAVIOR, CHRIST JESUS

Thank you, Jesus, for being God and man. I'm so grateful that he was God, because he saved me and delivered me from all my sins. The Bible says that no man can save only God through Christ Jesus can wash away sin and no one but God, through Christ Jesus brings you into the family of God.

No one but God, through Christ Jesus, gives us a divine privilege to be blessed just because of what he did and not because of what we've done. According to the Bible, all of our righteousness and our good deeds are as filthy rags.

All glory goes to God for sending His son to live, breath and walk on this earth amongst humankind. He came to seek and to save those who were lost. In John 10:10 he said, "I come that you might have life and that more abundantly." John 3:16-17 says that, "God so loved the world that He gave His only begotten son that whosoever believeth in him should not perish but have everlasting life. God sent not His son into the world to condemn the world, but that the world through him might be saved." In John 14:6, Jesus said, "I am the way the truth and the life…" John 10:9 quotes Jesus as saying, "I am the door… No man cometh unto the Father but by me…"

HE BECAME FLESH AND DWELT AMONG US

I'm also grateful that, even with his divinity, Jesus was a man so he could be touched with the feelings of our infirmities. He who knew no sin became sin that we might be the righteousness of God. The nature that we all have without Christ is sinful. Therefore, we needed a savior who could be touched; who would understand our frailties, our struggles and weaknesses. Jesus not only understands, but he also does something about our situations. He saves, he delivers and he heals from all manner of sickness and disease. Thank God that he can set us free; "Whom the 'Son' sets free, is free indeed" (John 8:36).

MY PERSONAL THOUGHTS ON CHAPTER 1

_____

_____

_____

_____

_____

_____

_____

_____

_____

_____

_____

_____

_____

_____

_____

_____

_____

CHAPTER 2

GOD'S ASSIGNMENT IS SPECIFIC

Isaiah 61:1; Luke 4:18; Jeremiah 1:1-7; 1 Samuel 16:1-13; Matthews 28:19-20

Avoid vision clutter because you might have a lot of good plans and ideas, but they may be for another season.

THE DIFFICULTY OF PRIORITIZING

It's a challenge to prioritize what's most important concerning your goals and what you are willing to sacrifice in order to obtain them. Many times, where you are in life can determine what's most important at that time. Be careful that you don't waste time investing in something that has nothing to do with where you're going. You could get stuck, and like in quick sand, you could go under. Timing is everything. Making wise choices by listening to wise counsel could prevent you from wasting energy, needless effort and unintentional embarrassment.

Vision clutter does not mean that you do not have good ideas and aspirations. Vision clutter can be overwhelming especially when there are so many great ideas you desire to implement at the same time. In that case, vision clutter will develop into mental clutter and become a tool of the enemy. All the ideas and aspirations in your heart and mind are tied to you, and believe it or not, you are tied to them. This is confusing and burdensome because you keep seeing what you can't make happen right now.

This is not of God, because the Bible states, "Be anxious for nothing…" (Philippians 4:6). Always remember that even if God gave you the vision, it is yet for an appointed time. It shall speak and not lie. Though it tarries, wait for it. It shall surely happen (Habakkuk 2:2-3).

You must write your vision and make it plain for yourself and for others. Literally, take the time to write your personal and/or spiritual vision down on paper, or type it on your computer, iPad, etc. Give yourself realistic time lines that you will be able to follow through with. This will help to remove vision clutter and relieve your mind from the constant agony of not being able to achieve your goal or vision in the "right now". It's okay at times to add to your goal or vision in order to bring more clarity to it. While waiting for the fullness of time, you might change some of your ideas and you might make some adjustments in the time lines you established.

The passage of time often brings new thoughts, ideas and better methods. Yet, if the baby is born prematurely, sometimes it will not be healthy! Writing or typing your vision or goal and adding to it from time to time is alright, as long as you can walk away from it knowing that it might not be for now; it might have to wait.

THE DILEMMA OF REMAINING FOCUSED

Even though you have become organized and you have prioritized your schedule and deadlines, there is yet the challenge of being able to stay focused on what you've written and planned to achieve on a daily basis. I believe that this is an ongoing fight on all levels of life, especially for those who are extremely busy and have a lot on their plates.

Busy people become busier, because they seem to have what it takes to handle more than others do. This can be a good sign, but it could be a bad sign as well. It's a good sign because people who can "multi-task" are always needed. Take for instance the single parent who raises children, somehow juggles going to school and manages working to be the best he or she can be for his or herself and for his or her family. This is awesome because it's so difficult to do. Hats off to those who have to make it work in life without the luxury of having the support of a companion to assist them.

How about all of those bills that stare us in the face? Bill collectors keep you in mind, no matter what your dreams and drives are. They're here to remind you what you owe and what you don't have to pay it back.

This is extremely frustrating because you want to take care of your responsibilities, but you're not making enough income to handle it all. This is definitely something that can take you off course and detour you from remaining focused. What the devil wants you to look at is where you are right now. He wants you to focus on your lack, your debt, your insecurities and your insufficiencies. He wants you to look at what people did to you and the mistakes that you made in the past. He wants you to dig a deep mental hole and live in it, so that you won't have the mental energy to find your way out.

That's why you have to fight to avoid being side tracked. You might find it easy to start to go in the right direction after being off course. However, in most cases, you'll find yourself being pulled unintentionally right back into another direction. At times we become side tracked because something appears to be the right thing to do at that moment. However, it may be the wrong thing to do for where we're trying to go.

There's danger in seeking approval and validation from others. Always check to see if the advice you're getting is overbearing or overly suggestive, because that type of advice is neither good nor healthy. Never listen to anyone who presses hard to alter what you should or should not do unless it's the Lord Himself confirming what you know is right or wrong to do. If it's the Lord, then it should serve as a reminder.

Be aware of people who are controlling. Controlling people who are extremely persuasive in their views can make you feel uncomfortable and vulnerable. If you're not careful, you'll make decisions based on someone else's directions. Remember, you must be persuaded by your own mind.

When the controlling person provides or tries to provide advice or counsel, thank the controlling person for his or her advice, and move on with what you know is right to do. Allow God to direct your life. You must stay open at all times but discern, through sound judgment, by the Holy Spirit. This is why it's most essential that you are a part of a strong Bible-believing church and actively involve yourself in Bible class. Your personal relationship with God comes through reading and studying the Bible on a regular basis. Psalms 119:105 says, "Thy word is a lamp unto (your) feet and a light unto (your) path." The Holy Spirit will lead and guide you into all truth.

It's good to listen to other people's testimonies and experiences in life, but it's dangerous to live by them. Learn from it even though you can't live by it; you must live by the word of God, which is the final authority and guide for living. Even practical advice must be based upon God's word. There is so much advice being given through the media that, if we are not careful, we will take the voice of the media as the final authority. How can someone teach you how to live when he or she has no clue how life should be lived from God's perspective? That's like "the blind leading the blind" and they will all fall into a ditch together.

You must become fully convinced that you have been ordained by God. The Bible states in Ephesians 4:27, "Neither give place to the devil." Satan knows that if you are not convinced within yourself that you are God's chosen, a door or a passage way is opened to deceptive, misleading plans and agendas. Divine confidence and assurance shuts the door to false prophets, demonic influences and the persuasive plans of the enemy. Philippians 1:6 should encourage and strengthen you, "Being confident of this very thing, that He which has begun a good work in you will perform it until the day of Jesus Christ."

THE DECIDING FACTOR OF FOLLOW-THROUGH

Mental and vision clutter cause us to want to immediately implement all of the many ideas and plans we have. It takes discipline to remain focused on implementing and completing the "right now" task(s). Once we've made the decision regarding what we are to do in a particular season, the next challenge is following the task through until completion.

I believe that we have a built in mechanism or drive that comes from God to complete tasks. At times, we need others to help motivate us, but ultimately, we must keep ourselves inspired to finish tasks. Like a track star, we must pace ourselves for the long haul. Setting the pace for a race is not easy, because each runner must establish, through practice, his or her initial pace. A runner also needs to know when to give it all he or she has as he or she gets close to the finish line. Pace setting can only be established through experiences in life and learning from previous mistakes.

When trying to build or put something together, time must be taken to read the directions to ensure that the right tools are in place and all of the parts are accounted for. If steps are skipped because they are deemed unnecessary, items could be put together incorrectly. Then, taking everything apart and starting all over again is inevitable. This is what happens when we rush and don't pace ourselves to make sure that we have what it takes to run in our races before we get started.

What happens when you feel like you ran well, but you were hindered? This is how some people feel when they don't understand why they didn't follow through on a project. Possibly, they were hindered because of a lack of knowledge. Hosea 4:6 says, "My people are destroyed for a lack of knowledge." This is a biblical principle that will never get old. It can be used from generation to generation. Any contractor or architect knows that he or she must keep the cost of a project in mind while thoroughly planning and investigating the completion of the task. They must explore all of the facts and details to determine if they have what it takes to follow through with completing the task.

THE DETERMINATION TO MAKE IT HAPPEN

Without determination, goals and/or visions will remain dreams and never become a reality. This is where many fail; they start off telling others about their goals and/or visions, but they never put legs to them. After a while, their conversations become boring or stale. People begin to mock them, saying "Yeah, yeah, yeah, we've heard this (or that) before." Sometimes people talk about their goals and/or visions so long without acting upon them that others view their conversations as null and void.

There are so many who have lost the drive to birth their dreams into reality. It's sad; like the grave yard, it's filled with those who had dreams but never saw them become reality. Some died with regret and unfilled desires, allowing life to take away their strength, determination and motivation. They gave up hope, saying, "What's the use? I don't have what it takes any more to make it happen." If that's you, I speak to your spirit and to your mind. Rise up and say with determined conviction, "Not me! I'm not going out like that! I shall live and not die to see the works of the Lord!" Psalms 92:13 says, "Those who are planted shall be fruitful again." In other words, when you are planted, you know the voice of God and you can avoid the deception of defeat. Jesus said, "My sheep know my voice and a stranger they will not follow."

The voice of God can be distinguished within our spirits. Some people encounter confusion that prevents them from distinguishing the voice of God from what is not God. If Satan can keep your head filled with conflicts and issues, you could get very distracted while trying to make destiny decisions. Satan makes every attempt to confuse and discourage positive endeavors.

Satan has so many deceiving methods and strategies that you definitely need to know when God is speaking. He speaks through His word and He speaks through personal devotion. You learn to recognize the voice of God by spending time talking with God in prayer, and spending time reading His word.

For example, when you develop a relationship with someone, you have to spend time talking and experiencing quality time with that person to really get to know them. Spending time with a person, looking into their eyes and communicating with them is the only way you will get to know what they like and don't like. You learn about them through spending time with them and listening to them. It is the same with God. You learn His likes and dislikes, His ways and His voice when you spend time with Him. When God speaks, He won't go against His written word. Be sure to judge everything you hear by the word of God. The Holy Spirit will teach you and guide you into all truth. Always trust God's word. Trust His spirit to be your guide through dark seasons when you don't know what to do.
Trust that God will give you direction in your personal life, and you will make it through any struggles.

Trusting God is a protective mechanism, a safety net for His people. God's safety net, our trust, is vitally important for our safety. We don't have time to waste trying to see if this is God or if that is God. To save time, always seek God. If you seek the kingdom of God and His righteousness, all these other things shall be added unto you (Matthew 6:33). Jeremiah 30:3 says, "Call on the Lord and He will answer and show you great and mighty things ye know not of."

Highly anointed and gifted vessels can fall in the trap of not seeking God in all aspects of their lives. I am a witness. I remember when I was much younger and I was seeking the will of God for my life. I desired companionship and wanted to know who my mate was, but because I loved God with all of my heart, I wanted to be in His will concerning who I would marry.

There was an incident where I was in someone's home and the person began prophesying to me concerning who I would marry. This Prophet stated that my future wife was a princess in Taiwan, and that she was waiting for me. The Prophet also described the physical appearance of the woman that was to be my wife. I was very upset about this. It disturbed me for a long time because I had such a heart for God, and I really believed His Prophets. Therefore, at that time, if a Prophet spoke and said, "Thus says the Lord" I believed it. I hadn't developed a strong relationship with the Lord for myself, so I depended upon those who had strong "gifts" to speak into my life for divine direction. This was dangerous because I left myself open to be misguided.

I will never forget how extremely disappointed and frustrated I was. I believed what the prophet said, but I had not met my mate. I gave this situation to the Lord. I made up mind that I wasn't going to worry about it any longer. I figured in God's timing, He would show me who my wife would be.

On Sunday, June 4, 1978, our church choir had an engagement at the Healing Temple C.O.G.I.C. in Chicago, IL. As we were waiting to be called on, the most gorgeous young lady walked to the microphone. She sang prior to our choir singing. Her name was Ms. Gloria Windom. It appeared as though I was so overtaken by her beauty and outward display of elegance, that I really wasn't paying attention to the song she was singing. The song was "He's So Real." Now that I look back, I probably thought she was singing about me. Of course, she was singing about Jesus. Ha! Ha! We met after the service and through God's awesome kindness, we came together and we were married on Saturday, August 2, 1980 at the Faith Temple C.O.G.I.C. in Chicago, IL. where the late Bishop H. W. Goldsberry was the Senior Pastor at that time. We've been married for thirty years and we are extremely happy, blessed and enhanced by each other's gifts and talents.

That is why I encourage God's people to be very careful whose homes they visit. Be wary of private in-home prayer meetings. They could be very dangerous because they could bring confusion to your life if you're not watchful. The older saints taught us to stay away from having home prayer meetings. I can say that I really saw for myself how damaging they could be. It's sad to say that some of these settings could be an open door and a trap for the devil himself to prey upon vulnerable, insecure seekers who have low self-esteem.

However, it would be different if a person has been given authorization by his or her Senior Pastor to hold an at-home outreach location for prayer meetings that follow the guidelines of the local church. Just the same, I would check with the Senior Pastor of that local church to hear for myself if that outreach location has the approval to have prayer meetings. This will only help to protect you from chaos and confusion.

Prophesy is a needed gift in the body of Christ to edify, to exhort and to comfort. It's an awesome gift, yet, if not used with much wisdom, it can definitely offend someone. Therefore, those who operate in this gift must be in prayer, constantly in the word of God and under spiritual authority.

Also, as a Prophet, one must be a member of a solid Bible-based, praying church. Every prophet must stay humble and teachable at all times, because he or she needs the other gifts for the sake of accountability. Prophets are to help bring clarity and correction, if needed. No man is an island. We need one another for the perfecting of the saints, for the work of the ministry and for the edifying of the body of Christ.

It is so important to know for yourself what God called you to do. In the early 70's, I felt God was bringing me to the knowledge of his purpose for my life, because I needed to know for myself what God really wanted me to do. Being the son of a Pastor who was over a Pentecostal church in the C.O.G.I.C. organization better known as the "Sanctified Church," it was assumed that I was automatically called by God to preach. However, I didn't want to do something based upon what everybody else felt I was called to do. This was a hard season in my life, because I didn't want to preach. I wanted to use my talent to bless God's people through music, by singing songs that would bless the body of Christ.

My mom and dad began praying for me, so that I wouldn't make the wrong decision and go in a direction where I'd miss my kairos - God's timing for what He called me to do. I was given an opportunity to travel, but it was at the wrong time. I would have been doing ministry, but I would have been away from my church. If I would have taken that offer, I would not have been in the right place at the right time. God's desire was for me to take on the office of Senior Pastor after my father went on to be with the Lord.

Thank God for praying parents, who could see further than I could.

I was raised in a safe haven, where prayer and fasting were experienced quite often. My father had us fasting and praying a lot. Three day fasts and shuts-in were a common part of our Christian lifestyle. Having a place of safety is a necessity, even if it's not with your biological or natural family. Make sure you have a strong church family and Pastor who's watching out for your soul.

The Apostle Paul wanted to make sure that young Timothy was headed in the right direction and building on a solid foundation of truth. The Apostle John told the believers in the early church in I John 4:1, "Beloved, believe not every spirit, but try the spirits whether they are of God..." The way that you try a spirit (the voice that you hear or the prophet that may speak to you) is by the word of God. The Apostle Paul asked the church of Galatia in Galatians 5:7, "...who hindered you that ye should not obey the truth?"

Knowing and doing what you're called to do in the appointed time and seeking wise counsel only matters if you complete the task God called you to do. Jesus said in Matthew 10:22, "And (you) shall be hated of all men for my name's sake: but he that (endures) to the end shall be saved."

MY PERSONAL THOUGHTS ON CHAPTER 2

_____

_____

_____

_____

_____

_____

_____

_____

_____

_____

_____

_____

_____

_____

_____

_____

_____

_____

_____

_____

_____

_____

_____

_____

_____

_____

_____

_____

CHAPTER 3

GOD DOES NOT MAKE MISTAKES

Job 23:10; Psalms 23:3; Psalms37:23; John 16:13

IT WILL TAKE A LIFETIME TO LEARN JUST A LITTLE SOMETHING ABOUT LIFE.

With the vast amount of information available about the many subject areas on Earth, we could not begin to know everything about life. Whatever we do come to know about what has been placed here on Earth and about life must be discovered over time. God would never make a planet for His children to live on and not provide enough resources to take care of them. God knows all and sees all, and there is no mistake in what He plans for His creation.

Job said, "He knows the way I take." Job didn't know what was ahead, but he knew that God did. The things that happened to Job were allowed by God. God knew what Job could take, because He made him. While Satan was "going to and fro in the Earth" God called Job to Satan's attention. God asked Satan, "Have you considered my servant, Job!" It appears as though God was bragging about Job to Satan. Wow! It's something else when God brags about you, but it also causes attention to be brought to you. People begin to notice you who never noticed you at other times. Job had everything going great in his life until he was noticed by both God and Satan.

Job's righteousness caused him to be recognized in the spirit realm. It also caused unexpected, unanticipated trouble to rise in his life. Job had to experience something he had not experienced in life, "trials and tribulations." His wealth was taken and his children were destroyed. His friends lost trust in him; his health failed him and his wife didn't support him or his God. Job had to follow a path that God knew. This was a strange season for Job, but he said, "…(God knows) the way that I take: when He (has) tried me, I shall come forth as gold."

While it's happening, suffering could appear as though God is making a mistake. However, God uses suffering to help us discover His goodness. Suffering is used to help us validate Him, to show us that He really has His hand of sovereignty on us at all times.

There have been so many times when I didn't know what to do or which way to go concerning my life. I needed God's help and guidance to assist me in my decision making processes. When I left the church organization that I was previously affiliated with, I was criticized, talked about and ridiculed for leaving the organization. However, I trusted God, and He held the church and I intact through all the storms that hit the ministry. When members began leaving during a series of transitions, some tried to tear down the ministry as they departed. It was heartbreaking to know that after I poured into people, they not only left the ministry, but also spoke against me and the work that I did for them. Thankfully, God held the church and I together through it all.

When the majority of the strong leaders departed, it appeared to have been a devastating period of time. I didn't know how I was going to make it with all new leaders. Nevertheless, God knows what we don't know. He knew that there were people anointed to step right in and help carry on the ministry. This was a time of adjustment for me. I had to learn new personalities and new styles of leadership. However, God gives us grace and the people required to help us accomplish what is needed in every season.

He is exact in all that He does. He is without flaw. I'm so grateful that God is God, and in control. With God, there's really nothing out of control, it just looks like it's out of control to us. There's nothing that happens that He doesn't know about. It's so encouraging to know that He is without flaw, yet He chooses flawed individuals to do His work on the earth. This is awesome because it means that He is capable of seeing us differently than we see ourselves. He sees us as strong, powerful and capable to do whatever He assigns us to do.

God is not surprised! Isn't that the way we feel at times? Don't we see ourselves differently than how God sees us? The issue is not that God isn't surprised. The issue is us being surprised about how God sees us. What a privilege it is to be seen by God as someone that can be used by Him! This is a powerful revelation and expression of love. 1 John 3:1 says, "Behold, what manner of love the Father hath bestowed upon us, that we should be called the sons of God…" That's why God chose us!

God knows why He chose you and you must rest and relax in His choice. There's something about you that's special to God. He made you fearfully and wonderfully. Did you know that you were made a little lower than the angels and that He has crowned you with glory and honor?

MY PERSONAL THOUGHTS ON CHAPTER 3

_____
_____
_____
_____
_____
_____
_____
_____
_____
_____
_____
_____
_____
_____

CHAPTER 4

GOD ALREADY KNOWS WHAT'S UP?

Jeremiah 29:11; Psalms 103:1; 2 Timothy 1:7

Trusting someone is good if it's someone who can be trusted. However, you must be careful that it's not the type of trust where you depend upon individuals for direction, instructions and/or for financial assistance all the time. This is not a healthy type of trust. When you rely on an individual for everything, you make that individual your source. Although we all need someone to be there to support us, befriend us and/or comfort us, we should never trust people with our existence. Further, we must be cautious when we look to our close friends for guidance. Remember, they are limited in their knowledge and they can't know everything. So make sure that you allow God, not man, to be your source. The Bible tells us not to put confidence in the flesh (in man), but to trust God. God wants us, His children, to live as though we have blindfolds on. Living life blindfolded means that when we walk by faith, we can't see where we're going, and we have to depend on God to take us where He wants us to go. I like this concept because when you are blindfolded, you have to rely on the perspective of the one who's leading you. We need the eyes of the Lord since it's His perspective, not ours, that we rely on when we lead blindfolded lives.

Leaving our perspective behind means that we have to shut down and ignore the facts as we see them, and walk in faith. If you don't learn this unusual concept for living as a Christian, then you will never live a victorious life as a Christian. We are faced with so many different things that challenge how we believe on a daily basis. The "natural man" has to deal with emotions, imaginations, physical challenges, social challenges and moral challenges. If we are not careful, these challenges will make us give up trying to live a successful life by faith. It literally takes the presence of God, the power of God and having the promises of God rehearsed in your ears over and over again to bring you to a place of acceptance of living by faith. You must learn how to have "childlike" faith and take leaps in life without having fear.

There is a personal experience that I reflect on when I consider "childlike" faith. One day my son, Donald II, who was about five years old at the time, came down the stairs of the church with me. The stairway was extremely steep because the sanctuary of the church was on the second floor. As I was coming down the stairs, I gripped Donald's hand. Being a child full of energy and loving to play, Donald was always risky and daring as a child. He still is! However, Donald did something that frightened me on that day. He caught me off guard because without any notice, he took a giant leap up into the air. I was somewhat afraid, but not Donald. He was fine. I remember saying something like, "Donald, be careful son." He replied, "Daddy, I'm alright because you've got my hand!" I will never ever forget that statement. God spoke to me through my son's statement. God's has our hands and we are safe in His hands!

Even when we take a leap in life and we don't know the outcome, we should always remember that God's got our hands. We are in the hand of God, and no matter what it looks like, we are safe in Him. It was Donald's "childlike" faith that taught his father a life lesson that can be applied to every situation that may arise.

MY PERSONAL THOUGHTS ON CHAPTER 4

_____
_____
_____
_____
_____
_____
_____
_____
_____
_____
_____
_____
_____

CHAPTER 5

GOD WON'T CHANGE HIS MIND BUT HE PLANS TO CHANGE YOURS
Philippians 2:5; Philippians 3:13-14; 2 Corinthians 10:3-4; Joshua 1:8-10; Psalms 1:2; Romans 12:1-2; Philippians 4:8

One hard truth about being chosen by God is that you're on His agenda whether you like it or not. Further, God has given us a free will, because He wants us to be willing vessels for His glory. God has a plan in mind for each of us, but how He intends to bring it to pass is sometimes beyond our understanding. Just admit it. We would prefer living our lives the way we want to live them without a pull from an inner voice or that daily reminder that we are supposed to be doing a specific thing. This can be very frustrating especially when we have our own goals and personal aspirations in mind.

Goal oriented people find it difficult to change their pursuits. However, they are "stubborn" enough to get where they desire to go and they are driven enough to obtain everything they want in life. When parents promote education and entrepreneurship as ways to become successful in life, it encourages individuals to become goal oriented. Goal oriented people are extremely focused and determined to fulfill their goals and aspirations. Some people might call them "prideful;" "heady;" or "high-minded." In their defense, many goal oriented people only reflect their determination through their body language and not through their words or actions toward others.

It's a good thing for an individual to have goals, determination, and the mental strength to achieve in life. With all of the fantastic things that goal oriented people can expect out of life, they must remember to acknowledge God in all of their ways. As we pursue our God given dreams during our lives, we must acknowledge God in all of our ways. He promised to direct our paths. Leaving God out of "the big picture" self inflicts heartache and pain. When we exclude God, we are like the person who is given a paint brush and never learns to paint. Inexperienced painters take the brush, strokes side to side, then up and down in an attempt to make something beautiful. This is unlike the experienced painter who uses the right strokes to get exactly what he or she wants to create on a canvas. We have a better chance of getting desired results with a skilled painter than with an inexperienced painter. If we are the inexperienced painter, we put ourselves at risk for a "messed up" personal canvas when we don't allow God to be involved with our goals and dreams. He is the master artist, creator and designer of our lives and He knows what to do with our lives.

I have been born again for over forty years. Being raised in the church, I was taught the word of God by my father, Dr. James B. Alford, Sr. He was a thorough teacher. He was also known throughout Christendom as one of the most respected teachers and preachers in the body of Christ. My father emphasized reading and studying the word of God. He was an advocate of buying books, especially Christian literature. He believed strongly that Christians are anchored in the biblical knowledge of Christ Jesus through hope and faith.

With all of the debris and filth that's presented to us on a daily basis, I see the necessity of studying the word of God for myself and the need to protect my mind. We must watch the thoughts that enter our minds. If we don't stay alert to the negative or filthy thoughts that come to our minds on a daily basis, we can be overtaken unaware. That's why Jesus told his disciples to, "Watch and pray!" Guarding our thoughts is not always easy because it takes changing the way we think.

Mental transformation is a necessary and an ongoing process. As we pursue the knowledge of God's word through prayer and study, we begin to change. However, we have to decide to be open to the Holy Spirit. The Holy Spirit will remove old concepts and thoughts while interjecting new thought and ideas. The Holy Spirit deals with us concerning every thought that enters our minds. He will check every thought. Nothing approaches us that the Holy Spirit won't deal with or warn us about. Negative and filthy thoughts grieve the Holy Spirit and take away from our liberty.

Demonic mental control comes to detour us through internal conflict or spiritual warfare. Spiritual warfare is not recognized with the natural eye. It's not the visual of an angel or a devil sitting on an individual's shoulders.

Spiritual warfare is when a believer in Christ Jesus has a battle between doing what's right and what's wrong. This battle can occur in various areas in a person's life. It often affects the individual mentally, physically, and spiritually. Therefore, the believer must trust what God's word says in order to combat beliefs and concepts that are evil. Most of all, the believer has to hold fast to the desire of gaining victory over the very presence of evil. 2 Corinthians 10:5 states that we must, "(Cast) down imaginations, and every high thing that exalted itself against the knowledge of God and bringing into captivity every thought to the obedience of Christ."

Satan utilizes mental control because he knows the mind is the control center of the body. The mind regularly processes all manner of information and determines what information it should store and what information it should discard. The old saints told us that an, "Idle mind is the devil's workshop." That is so true. Many people are deceived because they have difficulty focusing on positive activities and ideas. They become addicted to narcotics and/or fall into relationships that are ungodly. Some people even become stuck in sinful devices which they are unable to free themselves from. Mental transformation is a necessity because once our minds are renewed, we face challenges differently.

We all experience conflict as a result of spiritual warfare. It's sensed and felt emotionally although it's unseen. During spiritual warfare, God utilizes angelic assistance to aid us in our walk of faith. Unfortunately, there is also a demonic presence assigned to us at the same time. Demons are empowered to attempt to prevent us from becoming or doing what God has purposed for us. Therefore, surrendering ourselves over to God is an absolute necessity. You must refuse to be an enemy of God as a result of an ungodly thought life. Romans 8:7 says, "The carnal mind is enmity against God..." In other words, the mind can cause one to become an enemy of God through corrupt thinking and living. Isaiah 1:19 reports, "If (you are) willing and obedient, (you) shall eat the good of the land." Seeking to obey God by striving to think right is a part of truly accepting and not rejecting God's will for your life.

One of the worse things to do is to fight the will of God. When you are "out of" the will of God, it hurts you and causes harm to those who are under your guidance or authority. In essence, other people are affected by your disobedience. Ask Jonah! When Jonah paid his ticket to ride the boat to Tarish, there was a storm that almost killed everyone on the ship. After Jonah was tossed into the sea, the men were saved from inevitable destruction.

God allows us to make our own decisions in life. He orchestrates circumstances that cause us to see how much we really need divine direction and guidance in our lives. Pastor Darius Brooks wrote a song that simply says, "His will is what's best for me!" The safest place in the whole wide world is in the will of God. There is not a day or an hour that anyone should want to live outside of the safety of God's will. I encourage you to allow God, without difficulty or struggle, to change how you think. As previously referenced, "There is a way that (seems) right unto man, but the end thereof are the ways of death" (Proverbs 16:25).

God has a plan for your life and He challenges your way of thinking in order to change you. Even as believers, we have a daily fight against evil. We cannot afford to trust in our own abilities to win on the "battlefields" of our minds, because there is no good thing within us. Job 14:1 tells us, "Man that is born of a woman is of few days, and full of trouble." Whatever thoughts you allow to control your mind will also control your life! Hence, our thoughts can determine life or death for us. Our thoughts can bring us to a "dead end" or to an abundant life in Christ Jesus, our Lord. This is an alarming truth, but the Bible reminds us that, "the wages of sin is death; but the gift of God is eternal life through Jesus Christ our Lord" (Romans 6:23). The sooner we allow change to occur in our lives, the quicker we can move forward in life.

We love to blame others for our failure to move ahead in life. We find ourselves saying, "No one understands what I've been through." Get over yourself and move on with your life! Sometimes it's hard, but you have to get to a point where you just, "Get up!" If you don't "get up", then you will "live down" or beneath your purpose. You will sit right where you are, with the same state of mind, blaming others for where you are.

I don't know anyone who's anointed and chosen by God to do effective ministry who hasn't gone through some painful experiences in life. Nobody can avoid pain, disappointments and setbacks. This means that situations are going to hurt at times. Yes, there will be some shame on the journey. However, it's all a part of our Christian lives. We must deny ourselves, take up our crosses and follow Jesus.

I believe God doesn't want us to ignore the experiences in our lives. He wants us to learn from our experiences, so we can avoid making the same choices. He also desires that we help prevent others from making some of the mistakes we've made.

Intentional hurt in our lives is not acceptable. Hurts that were brought into your life, through no fault of your own, are not acceptable. Anyone who tells you that intentional hurt should be embraced is a liar and the truth is not in him or her. People who intentionally hurt you are definitely wrong for hurting you. However, it's over, and you've got to move on with your life. Guess what? It's your turn to have another chance to live. It's not too late to live again and to be restored in every area of your life. This is the day that the Lord has made and we need to rejoice and be glad in it (Psalm 118:24).

Believe it or not, it's God's love that is chasing after you. He's pursuing you with His love and mercy. He loves you so much that He doesn't want to leave you the way you are. Your existence is not at a level that you once saw and believed. You've been sad too long. You've grieved too long. You've been stuck in the same place too long. It's time to enjoy life again. God wants you to respond as a child does. He doesn't want you to have a care in world. His will is that you be relieved of the pressures and stresses of life. He wants you to cast your cares on Him because he cares for you. You are in the midst of a "love battle." "Love is fighting over you and for you!" I beg you to let God win! Often we are the enemies of God's plan for our destinies. Therefore, if the devil can sway us to from doing things God's way, we will become our own roadblocks for mighty achievements.

God's word is the avenue for mental regulations. In John 15:3 Jesus said, "Now are ye clean through the word which I have spoken unto you." Joshua 1:8 explains that we should keep the word of God in our mouths and we should always meditate (read, ponder, pray and contemplate) on the word. When the believer meditates on the word, he or she is grounded in the word. Psalm 1:3 says that the believer who meditates day and night is "...like a tree planted by rivers of water...and whatsoever he (or she) does shall prosper."

Listening to what God says and meditating on it could be challenging. However, if we think about God's word consistently, day and night, His words will be rehearsed in our minds. God watches over and protects His word. His word is what activates the power to bring things to pass. Having the mind of Christ endows us with power. This power shifts you far away from small thinking. It also causes you to believe that you can actually become more than what you were possibly raised to believe. God's word will change your mind set and you will gradually move from merely existing to living life to the fullest.

God's word becomes a part of your thought life after you spend time listening and pondering what He says. As you consistently study and meditate on God's word, His word will eventually begin to take root in your mind. The word of God is like a seed that needs to be sown into the ground. The ground in this case is our heart which affects our minds or our thoughts. Seeds, after being sown, need to be nourished and watered. They also need sunlight. During this process, roots begin to anchor themselves in the ground. Like literal roots, the word of God will take root in your mind and anchor itself after it receives constant nourishment.

The seed and the roots have a direct connection. The seed is meaningless without roots and the roots come from the seed that was sown. Therefore, they both have significant importance in relation to what is produced. Through this example, God is showing us that we need His word and that His word must be anchored in us in order to achieve His purpose for our lives.

The seed not only releases roots that anchor into the ground (or our hearts), but the seed also grows a stem which is a sign or evidence of growth. The stem is assigned to come out of the ground and to exist above the ground. It is susceptible to weather conditions and possibly to animals and insects. There can be no productivity if the stem does not spout out of the ground. After the stem is formed, then branches will extend from the stem. Leaves and flowers will form on each branch. Then, fruit will form on the branches. This is a necessary process for the development of fruit. Fruit must be nourished and cultivated before it can provide sustenance. We are the fruit. We have to grow and receive nourishment before we can provide nourishment and edification for others. This is what happens when we allow mental transformation to take place in our lives. It may take some time, but we will change.

MY PERSONAL THOUGHTS ON CHAPTER 5

_____

_____

_____

_____

_____

_____

_____

_____

_____

_____

_____

_____

_____

_____

_____

_____

_____

_____

_____

_____

_____

_____

_____

_____

_____

CHAPTER 6

GOD HAS A DESIGNATED TIME TO WORK WITH YOU

Ecclesiastes 3:1; Hebrews 9:27; Psalms 31:15

Time is an agent for God because He defines eternity. God makes the appointments in our lives; therefore, the timing in our lives is in His hands. One thing I love about God is that time, by our standards, doesn't appear to matter. It may appear to be late to us, but somehow He knows how to redeem the time. God supernaturally orchestrates things in our favor. Favor is not fair. Anything that held us captive in former seasons will not be capable of hindering us when God speaks and changes the time and the season. Demons cannot operate the same way that they operated in previous seasons. God allowed certain trials to come in former seasons that He won't permit to come into your new season.

I recall a conversation with my father a few months before he went home to be with the Lord. He said, "Son, you won't have to go through the things that I went through. It will be different for you, it will be easier." My father recognized from a spiritual perspective, through prophetic eyes, that time would bring about a change for the ministry and for me. I can say that this is what actually happened. It was as though the challenging personalities in my father's ministry were different when I became Pastor. I guess we can say time brings about change!

Time is an agent that is greatly used by God to fulfill a divine purpose for each of us towards a bigger picture called "The Kingdom!" God wants His kingdom to come and His will to be done on earth as it is in heaven. The Father sincerely desires that His righteousness reign forever here on earth. The kingdom of God is the reign and rule of God on earth and in the lives of each believer who's in Christ Jesus. We are destined to walk in divine authority through Christ Jesus as Adam once did. The failure to use our time correctly can be dangerous and costly. We cannot afford to waste time. Time brings each of us to all that God has planned and ordained for us to be in this life according to His purpose.

In the Garden of Eden, the serpent came to Eve. Then, Eve came to Adam and deceived him. Satan knew that time was of the essence; he had to quickly cause Adam and Eve to be separated from the reality of being one before God. There was a unique union between them, one that man has never been able to have with God since.

Our loving Father sent His son Jesus to dwell on earth and to pay the penalty for all of man's sin. Jesus also came to free us from the condemnation, shame and eternal destruction that we deserved. As a result of His love, He came and straightened the messed up situation that Adam caused for us. This was accomplished through his son, Jesus.

The sooner you walk in your destiny, the better it is for you and those who are connected to you. "Why put off until tomorrow what you can do today," is an old saying. There is so much truth in that statement. Everybody wants to be able to go to the bank, put money in today and the same day or within a few days, get a return on their investment. However, it doesn't quite work like that, although it would be wise to start investing in your future today. Stop saying, "I'll get around to it." This can be a cycle you've created that you can get stuck in for the rest of your life, if you're not careful. You'll say, "I wish I'd done this or that a little sooner." Some people regret their years of procrastinating. But we can't cry about yesterday's mistakes. Shame on you, if you don't learn to do something about it today! This is the day the Lord has made, let us rejoice and be glad in it (Psalm 118:24)!

We have an excellent opportunity to rise up and do what the Apostle Paul said, "…forgetting those things which are behind, and reaching forth to those things which are before, I press toward the mark for the prize of the high calling of God in Christ Jesus" (Philippians 3:13-14). Satan came to take away quality time. He came to steal, kill and destroy. He wants to make you feel that your life is a waste, but it's not!

You are fearfully and wonderfully made and Psalms 8:5 says, "For thou hast made (you) a little lower than the angels, and hast crowned (you) with glory and honor." What manner of love the Father hath bestowed upon us that we should be called, "the sons of God."

Don't waste another day over foolish stuff; it's not worth your time. It's a shame that some people make other people their lives because they don't have lives of their own. When you allow another person's life to become yours, then you're not living according to the purpose for which God, the creator, created you. There will be confusion and total unrest all the days of your life. Irritation and conflicts will go on between you and others because of disagreements, especially if you're constantly trying to please and satisfy others. This was not meant to be achieved amongst humans, because we were created in God's image for His glory.

When you get so involved in other people's affairs and ignore what God told you to do, you may be doing a good thing, but is it what God told you to do? If it's not, then it's foolish and a complete waste of time. Only what you do for Christ will last! Jesus always told the people that he was there to do the will of the Father. He made it quite plain. Any time we get involved in making others' desires and wishes first on our agendas, we are out of the will of God.

No one knows the day or the hour in which Jesus will appear, but we better be found doing the will of the Father when he comes. None of us has any time to waste, because none of us knows when he will come again or return for us through death. That's why it's extremely important to move forward with the preparation process for your assignment. Your intentions may be good, but it's not good if you don't ever do what you intended to do.

It's sad to live life working a secular job and never doing your God-given job! What will you say when you stand before God? All of us have to stand before the judgment seat of Christ to give account of those things we accomplished on earth. All of us must prepare to meet our God, face to face! But the question is, what will you say to Him when He calls your name? If He has a mandate upon your life to use you for a specific purpose, then please do what He has chosen for you to do!

MY PERSONAL THOUGHTS ON CHAPTER 6

_____

_____

_____

_____

_____

_____

_____

II. THE METHOD OF DEVELOPMENT

CHAPTER 7

GOD'S METHOD OF PERSUASION

Jonah 1:1-17; Jonah 2: 1-10; Psalms 139:8; Matthew 24:1-5

It's easier to accept the call of God and go through preparation without delay. Many people have negated the fact that time is of the essence concerning the call of God. They have been persuaded by carnal attractions, worldly connections and "soul-ties" which cause inner bondage. All of these involvements are part of a deceptive plan designated and orchestrated by Satan himself. His purpose is to deceive the very elect, if possible. We are living in an hour of deception in which we, as believers, must watch and pray like never before. If the acceptance of the call is delayed, it will not only delay the fulfillment of the assignment, but it will also delay God's promises for your life.

The call is not worth putting off because of the fear of not being able to fulfill your call. Trust me; it's easier to accept the call than to run from the call. Running from the call will only bring heartache and pain. Chosen people have a difficult time trying to abort their assignments. Some people may not want to admit it, but it's a real truth. First of all, you are called to something that you don't even feel qualified to do. Second, you have to deal with your own insecurities and inward weaknesses. Third, you have to minister to people who have many personal challenges, and they expect you to give them the answers to their problems. So, while you going through what you're going through, you have to minister to others. Let me be honest: it's very difficult! After having many experiences trying to handle all of the challenges and all of the complex situations that come with the call, you will find that it was never accomplished by you or your natural ability. The call was designed by God to be carried out only by the Grace of God. It's His power and ability that makes the responsibility of your call happen through you. God told Zerrubabel, in Zechariah 4:6, "...Not by might, nor by power, but by my spirit, (says) the Lord!"

I admit that it takes time to learn how the call functions through you and not by you. As humans, we are used to attempting to handle problems the best way we can on our own. There's something within our human nature that doesn't want to rely on God's way of working situations out for us.

I know waiting to see the avenue that God will open for us gets on our "last nerve" at times. However, God knows that through the waiting, He's building character. The waiting also builds a trust within our hearts as never before. It's through waiting that we find out who we really are and what is really best for us. We ought to thank God for allowing us to wait for Him, because we would have gotten into some destructive situations if not for the Grace of God.

Chosen people have chosen challenges that are tools to learn from. If I could have met with God to see my future and to discuss what I was called to do, I would have possibly selected something different. I would have begged God to give me another assignment, or asked if I could avoid the challenges that I foresaw in my life. I believe I'm speaking for all of us who've been through unspeakably painful experiences that only God knows about.

As you travel on this road of life, you will run into potholes, bumps and ditches. Another person may even throw the garbage out of his or her window that will fall right in front of your pathway. You'll need good driving or walking skills to avoid distractions or road blocks. You must be alert at all times! There are many issues that may occur on the road while you're travelling, but it's all a part of life and you must remain alert to avoid destruction.

God will allow all things to work together for our good. I never understood and I yet don't know how God uses all things. I understand His use of some things, but not all things. This is a mind boggling truth. That's why He's God and we're not. He can take red blood and wash away black, dirty, filthy sin and make us white as snow! His ways are not our ways and His thoughts are not our thoughts. His ways are past finding out!

All situations and circumstances, no matter how horrible they are, somehow work within the pre-destined plan of God, and good will come out of them. He allowed Satan to touch Job's life without killing Job. It was devastating when Job lost all of his children. It was "gut wrenching" for Job to lose all of his wealth. It was cold for his so-called friends not to support him during his time of trial. It was awful to have to deal with being attacked physically, to face embarrassment and to carry an odor. Job's wife left and didn't have anything good to say to him. Her question to Job was, "Why don't you curse God and die?" Wow! That came from his wife. Yet, God permitted all of these things to happen to Job. God gave Satan permission to touch his stuff, his family, his body and his relationships. However, after Job prayed for his friends, he recovered and God gave him back double for his trouble. The Lord blessed the latter end of Job more than his beginning (Job 42:12). Job acquired more wealth than he had before the trial.

This is such a great story for us to reflect on. It deals with losing and with regaining what was lost. All of us have lost things and loved ones, but it's good to know that God is a "Sovereign" God. He has a plan to restore us with better relationships and greater opportunities in life. God never intended for Job to die without having a testimony of recovery. After all Job went through, he was given double the amount of wealth that he had in the beginning. What a great lesson to learn from. Never give up! Expect what tomorrow brings. Live each day with an attitude of expectancy. Keep living and looking for God's best to show up in your life.

Do not put others in harm's way because of your disobedience. Jonah's disobedience almost caused others to be placed in harm's way. The people on his boat almost died. In Jonah's avoidance of his assignment, he thought for some reason that he could go into other directions. Well, isn't that how we feel at times? You may be trying to avoid your calling while you're reading this book, doing everything you can to go in another direction. However, God will not change His mind concerning your calling. No matter what you try to do, your call is still the same whether you like it or not. You can move out of town, change addresses or even change jobs, but your calling is still the same.

It's dangerous to be around those who are walking in disobedience. You may be experiencing hits and blows because of the disobedience of somebody close to you. Jonah eventually recognized his disobedience and told the people on the ship to throw him over board after the lot fell on him. God revealed why the storm appeared through the throwing down of the lots and through calming the storm after Jonah was cast overboard. Once they threw him overboard, there was a great calm in the atmosphere, on the sea and onboard.

Overlooking disobedience always causes a ruckus in our lives. Obedience always brings about peaceful results. So whatever you do, accept what God allows. Embrace His method of development because it is designed to bless you and others.

MY PERSONAL THOUGHTS ON CHAPTER 7

_____

_____

_____

_____

_____

_____

_____

_____

_____

_____

_____

_____

_____

_____

_____

_____

CHAPTER 8

GOD'S ENABLING ABILITY THROUGH LOVE

Romans 1:16; Judges 2:1; John 3:16-17; John 13:34-35

God has an everlasting love for us, and He will never break His covenant with us as His children. It is comforting to know that no matter how many times we've blown it and walked contrary to His will, God yet loves us. The true meaning of unconditional love should never be demonstrated to unworthy people, such as you and I, but that's what makes Him God!

Psalm 103:13, says "…as a father pities his children, so the Lord pitied them that fear Him." In other words, a real father doesn't chastise his children harshly for everything that they may do. A real father handles each situation differently. That's what God, our Father, does concerning His children. Now that we are cleansed through the blood of Jesus, God's son, God now sees us holy through His son and He doesn't respond in anger or wrath.

God doesn't respond like man. His love will continue to seek you out. God is like a hunter who wants His prey, so He must be very patient. If He's going to get the attention of His prey, God, like the hunter, must make wise moves. His timing must be correct when He makes His move. God said in His word that He came to seek and to save those who were lost. He has patience as well as the ability to seek us out. He knows where we live and what's on our agendas.

He knows our likes and dislikes; nothing surprises God. He's slow to anger and plenteous in mercy.

That's what I love about God. He will allow road blocks and setbacks to participate in the process of seeking us out. Sometimes He has to close a door while we're traveling, so it can appear as a detour to get us back on track. But if you think about it, aren't you glad that He closed some doors in your life just to get you back on track? God loves His children even when they make the wrong choices. A real parent just doesn't give up on his or her children just because of their disobedience. How many times have our children done us wrong and done others wrong? We keep right on claiming them as our children despite their wrong doings. Well, that's the way the Father in heaven treats us. Sometimes we don't walk according to God's will, but He helps to guide us and to keep us in the center of His will.

I'm so glad that God doesn't respond like man. It would be horrifying to know that every mistake we've made, depending on how people felt about it, would determine our punishment. Wow! That would be awful, because man doesn't have the heart, the mind or the ability within himself to really comprehend how to truly forgive someone else. Man can't do it because true forgiveness comes through the power of God. God is the only one that can "let us off the hook." He's the only one that can give us the heart to forgive someone who's done us wrong. I'm so glad that God didn't leave man in charge as judge to say "yes or no" to our eternal outcomes.

Allow God to love you to life. This sounds very easy, but it's not, because you must surrender your will over to Him. Otherwise, you will be working against God's love, which came to deliver and heal you. His love is on assignment to minister to your whole man. He wants to enter your life, and I mean every part of your life. He wants to deal with what needs to be dealt with in our hearts. He wants to reveal what's important and what's not important. God only wants what's best for us. Unconsciously, we can make "the cares of this life" more important than God. God knows our hearts. God's word says, "Man looks on the outward appearance, but God looks on the heart" (1 Samuel 16:7). In Matthew 6:21 Jesus said, "…where your treasure is, there will your heart be also." Always remember, God desires to see us do what He's predestined us to do. He also wants to bless our entire lives both naturally and spiritually.

In Revelation 3:20, God said to the Laodicea church, "Behold, I stand at the door, and knock: and if any man hear my voice, and open the door, I will come in to him and sup with him, and he with me." He knocks, but He doesn't tear the door down. His love causes him to knock and knock and knock. My question to you is, "How long will you allow Him to keep knocking and not open the door?" He is a gentleman. He gently pursues, but it's ultimately the choice of man to receive or reject His will. However, His spirit will leave in grief when His love is ignored. Don't allow the Holy Spirit to become grieved because you won't open up your heart and let Him in.

No one can stop God from loving us, no matter what we've done. God loves us just because He wants to! I know it's not a good reason, but it's the truth. God so loved the world that He gave His only begotten Son to be bruised for our iniquities, wounded for our transgressions, despised and rejected, acquainted with grief and with sorrow and whipped and beaten. Well, that doesn't make sense either, but God simply decided to show His love towards all of us. That's why He sent His Son. Jesus was sent to die for our sins so that we can all be saved if we believe that he is the Son of God.

God knew that man blew it because of Adam, but He made it possible for man to be rescued from destruction through Christ, the blood of Jesus. His love extends beyond understanding. I love that while we were yet sinners, Christ died for us! This goes way past what we've done or what we'll ever do. He loved us before we were even born and He loves us unconditionally. He loves us even if we don't love ourselves. He loves us even if others don't love us. We are yet loved by God, no matter what. We can't do enough wrong to make Him stop loving us.

If we reject Him unto death, His heart would be saddened. It would sadden him to know that those whom He loved rejected Him and chose to die and to live forever in the devil's hell, even though hell was not designed for us. God's love will go on forever for all humanity. He does not condone sin, but He does forgive those who have sinned. God hates sin, because it makes individuals live against the will of God for their lives. Sin is the transgression of the law. Sin causes an individual to seek only to please himself or herself and not others. Sin portrays a self-centered life style. It reflects a "me, myself and I" syndrome. Everything that Satan uses to deceive mankind is based upon what satisfies self, whether it's money, fleshly appetites, lustful desires, alcohol, drugs or sex.

Some goals are extremely selfish. Lies, greed, pride, gossip, strife and envy can be attributes of individuals with carnal desires. Those who seek academic achievements for the wrong reasons will not be completely satisfied. If we view this properly, we'd be surprised at all we do in life from self-centered aspirations and motivations. Even though you may be caught up in these types of self-centered sins, you can yet be forgiven. God forgives sin; 1 John 1:9 says, "If we confess our sins, He is faithful and just to forgive us our sins, and to cleanse us from all unrighteousness."

Guilt and condemnation hold individuals captive. You'd be surprised how many people actually live in this painfully agonizing state or condition of the mind. It is tormenting to wake up every morning to another day in shame because of something you've done in your past. Satan has tremendous opportunities to keep your past before you, because you've allowed him the place and the space to bring mental filth, again and again, into your mind. You must wake up and stop allowing the "accuser of the brethren" to keep messing with your head. Stand up to him with God's word and speak the word of the Lord over your life each day.

Romans 8:1 states, "There is therefore now no condemnation to them which are in Christ Jesus, who walk not after the flesh, but after the spirit." This means that when you accepted Jesus Christ into your life, you were immediately forgiven and born again. Your sins were washed away forever. God doesn't even remember them. So, tell Satan that you've been forgiven, that God has forgotten your sins and there's no truth to what he's saying to you anymore. You are saved, delivered and free forever. He did it because He loves you and plans to do great things in and with your life.

You need to accept the Gospel of Jesus Christ since it's the power of God unto salvation. The Apostle Paul said, "...I am not ashamed of the Gospel of Christ: for it is the power of God unto salvation to everyone that (believes)..." Through the preaching of the gospel, we are saved. Not by the works of our own are we saved, but by the grace of God we are saved. It's that simple: we hear, we believe and we receive. Supernaturally through the power of God's word, salvation takes place and our sins are washed away forever.

This process is necessary if we're going to be used as vessels for God's purpose.

MY PERSONAL THOUGHTS ON CHAPTER 8

_____

_____

_____

_____

_____

_____

_____

_____

_____

_____

_____

_____

_____

_____

_____

_____

_____

_____

_____

_____

_____

CHAPTER 9

GOD'S CHANNEL OF PREPARATION: TRANSITION

Jeremiah 18:1-6; Deuteronomy 8:1-3

In order for you to receive the spirit of "new," the spirit of "old" must go. I clearly understand, from a religious perspective, that once you are born again you have a new spirit and old things or sins are passed away and all things have become new in your spirit.

In Christ, we have *a position and a promise* that will take us where God wants us to be in life. Our position is our acceptance into the family of God. He calls us friends of God. He calls us sons of God. He also calls us "heirs of God" and "joint-heirs" with Christ Jesus. He said that we are seated with Him in heavenly places because of Christ Jesus. It's absolutely phenomenal that He sees us cleansed, forgiven and justified, through His son Jesus. Jesus died to make it possible for all humanity to be saved. In addition, it's a tremendous thing to know that God gave us a promise. God had an agreement with man that showed man what was expected of him in order to be "righteous." This was the "old covenant." The old covenant was difficult for man to live up to because it was based upon man's works or efforts. God knew that man could not live up to that level of perfection without the love of Jesus Christ dwelling within him. Therefore, God established a "new covenant" which could only be received by faith in Jesus Christ. The new covenant includes us, as His children, who are born again believers in Christ Jesus. He adopted us and gave us precious promises that we can stand on. He's not like some fathers who say they're going to do something and never follow through. He is capable of fulfilling what He promises and He will definitely bring what He says to pass.

However, the problem that we all have is not being properly positioned in Christ Jesus. As a result, we are not grateful and we do not rejoice over what has been promised to us. The real issue is the *pressure* before the fulfillment. It's the hell that we have to go through in order to obtain the promises. Most people don't know how to endure hardness like a good soldier; therefore, they fail. There is so much frustration within our hearts because we have the knowledge that God wants to do wonderful things with our lives, but we don't have the strength or character to endure the tough times.

Tough times cannot be ignored, as they are God's channels for the development of character. God uses tough times or pressure to work on our characters. It is through this channel called "pressure" that the soul actually reveals how strong or weak an individual is. It also identifies if we are truly ready for the next level of living. In addition, it pushes us to make destiny decisions in order to graduate to the next level.

Hard places are tests that come to see what we've learned as Christians. It's one thing to learn about the Bible and what it says; it's another thing to see if what we've learned actually works. Practical application is the key.

Without tests and trials, you will not be able to see the power of God in operation in your life. The various situations that you face from day to day bring about challenges to your faith. Faith must be challenged. Without challenges, we don't qualify for all that God has for us. If we endure challenges or "stand", it enables God's grace to be revealed in and through us. It also says to the Father that His child can handle an even greater blessing. It is God's grace that's sufficient and made perfect in our weaknesses. The reality of this truth is that our weaknesses must be discovered through our individual study of the word of God.

Old memories have a tendency to linger even after the things the memories were based upon are gone. There are certain ties to memories, people or situations that must be dealt with. This is where a constant battle in the mind, the will and the heart takes place. You can't take all of the memories, people and situations from your past into your future. These ties could hinder your future, and most of all, the purpose God intended for you. If you don't understand this, you will not be able to live your daily life victoriously. This is no joke; it's a walk of faith! You have got to dare to believe that God has something great in store for your life.

It's definitely a process that we must all go through if we're ever going to become all that God ordained us to be.

Allow for *mental adjustments.* This is essential, but changing your mind set will not be an overnight alteration. There are so many things that an individual experiences that have an effect on him or her. No matter who is right or wrong in a situation, we are affected in one way or another. Some effects are devastating while others are not. At times, our bodies are affected. The body is a horrible place to be affected by situations and circumstances. Doctors spend countless hours searching and seeking ways to cure individuals who suffer from different incurable diseases. The mental state has been a major area of concern, especially with so many people dealing with mental diseases, such as Alzheimer's and Dementia. There's research being done in these areas, but you'd be surprised by how many physical ailments and emotional challenges people face just because they won't make mental adjustments. Mental adjustments are absolutely necessary for our physical health, mental health, spiritual health and our overall well being.

If there's no change in your mind, there will be no change in your life. Deliverance has a whole lot to do with how one thinks. Jesus said to the man who was crippled for a long time, "Wilt thou be made whole?" (John 5:6). This man had a condition or ailment for thirty-eight years. Not only was he crippled in his limbs, he was crippled in his mind. Jesus dealt with his mental state first, and then he dealt with his physical state. Jesus said, "Rise, take up (your) bed, and walk" (John 5:8).

The devil cripples many people in their minds, causing "mental paralysis." Mental paralysis stops a person from moving forward in his or her life, because he or she is mentally chained to things. Some people are chained to garbage from their past. Garbage from the past oppresses the mind, hinders the will and strangles the desire to thrive in life. This not only affects the individual, but it also affects those who are around him or her. There is another term that can be used for this. It's called, "mental clutter."

As stated in a previous chapter, mental clutter means that you have so much on your mind that nothing gets accomplished. Some of the things on our minds are good and some are not. Therefore, we need to get rid of the stuff that's not good, so we can focus on the good things, no matter how difficult it is. One of the most frustrating things about mental clutter is trying to consistently stick with the principle of keeping a healthy thought life. We are all confronted with situations, circumstances and challenges on a daily basis, so maintaining healthy thoughts can be complicated. When you're enduring challenges, you need to establish biblical principles in your heart that will elevate your thinking. With a cluttered mind, we remain frustrated because we fail to send health to our thoughts. Every goal will seem challenging to accomplish with a cluttered mind. I found out that it's necessary for people to take breaks and to get away. A time of rest and replenishing aids in sending health to the physical body and to the mind.

There should be a balance of play with work. This may not sound spiritual, but we need to laugh and have good healthy fellowship with like-minded people. Great fellowship and lots of healthy laughing will help lift your mental state, especially while you are searching and seeking ways to birth what God has placed within you. The Bible tells us, "A merry heart doeth good like a medicine: but a broken spirit drieth the bones" (Proverbs 17:22).

Never be closed-minded. Closed-mindedness not only keeps out bad stuff, it also keeps out destiny tools. For example, God may desire to bring something to you through someone that you don't like or who you don't want to be bothered with. This can be dangerous, because the Bible tells us to be aware of how we entertain strangers, because we could be entertaining angels unaware (Hebrews 13:2). So, in order to remain open to potential destiny tools and positive information, you must be able to discern if it's God or not. You can discern whether it's God or not if you measure it against the word of God. The Holy Spirit will lead and guide you into all truth (John 16:13). Rely on His ability to lead you in the path of righteousness for His name's sake. There's too much at stake for us to be gullible and not depend on the Holy Spirit to guide us. People have been misled and wounded because they didn't depend upon the Holy Spirit to guide them. Some misled and wounded people even refuse to go to church because they did not discern properly.

An interesting part of transitioning is confronting every area of your life. I believe that this is possibly one of the most challenging areas, because God is dealing with you as you confront your areas of weakness. Admitting the truth about you to yourself is not easy. If you are dealing with self-esteem issues, it's even more difficult because you strive daily to feel good about yourself in all areas. When God starts to chasten and prune you, it isn't comfortable at all. No one really wants to see the true "self", if the truth be told.

Human nature would have us believe that because we're educated, have degrees and live pretty well with good incomes and prosperous businesses, that we're okay. We are tricked into thinking that our achievements define who we are and determine our self-worth. However, to God, accomplishments and scholastic achievements do not earn you the right to escape the "Potter's House." At the potter's house, vessels are made and reshaped for use. Each vessel requires a different shape to serve a different purpose. Therefore, while the potter is working on the wheel, he pulls and stretches to shape the vessel into a form where it can best serve its purpose. That's why we can't compare ourselves with others, and wonder why they didn't have to go through the things that we went through. They were designed to serve different purposes than us. You had to go through the situation that you went through because of the particular customized purpose assigned to your life.

Self-confrontation is necessary in order for spiritual surgery to be performed on the heart. We must reveal to God and to ourselves what were are facing within our hearts. This is crucial for true deliverance to take place, for out of the mouth the heart speaks. You must confess to the Lord with your mouth your sins, your weaknesses and your dilemmas. God said that if we confess our sins, He is faithful and just to forgive our sins, and to cleanse us from all unrighteousness (1 John 1:9).

The Lord wants all of us to allow the Holy Spirit to have open access to our lives in every area. If we really want Him to have open access to our lives, He will then come into our lives and begin to reveal every area that needs to be cleaned up.

Remember, "There is a way that (seems) right to man, but the end thereof are the ways of death" (Proverbs 14:12). This goes to show you that in our own sight as humans, we think so differently than God thinks. We're quick to say we're alright and that everyone has his or her own way of doing things. This is a carnal response when dealing with how we think and live. The Bible says a carnal mind is enmity against God (Romans 8:7). God hates carnal thinking because it deceives us and leads us into destruction. Be honest with yourself. Admit to God and to yourself that you need the help of God and the help of others who will support you.

Change is the only way to advance naturally and spiritually. Without it, we won't be able to become all that God ordained us to be. That means your associations and your environments must change. What you read, view on TV and the music you listen to must all be taken into consideration for change. But, as the saying goes, "Don't throw the baby out with the bath water." Consider change in any areas that do not assist you in moving forward toward a healthy and productive life in Christ Jesus.

Do whatever you must do and endure whatever you've got to endure to get to the promises of God.

MY PERSONAL THOUGHTS ON CHAPTER 9

_____
_____
_____
_____
_____
_____
_____
_____

CHAPTER 10

GOD'S PURPOSES CAN ONLY BE FULFILLED THROUGH TRANSITIONING

Joshua 1:1-5; Romans 8:28; Job 14:1

You will never get something different if you don't do something different. I'm sure you've heard that statement many times. If you want apples, then apple seeds must be planted in order to get an apple tree. This is a law that's established by God. All that God made from the earth had to reproduce itself after its kind (Genesis 1:11-12). Therefore, seeds were already within fruit, so fruit could reproduce itself by growing trees after its kind. When God created different fruit trees, they all had different seeds for individual purposes.

If Adam wanted apples, he would go to the apple tree to get apples. If Eve wanted grapes, she would go to the vine that grew grapes, and that's what she'd get. "First natural, then spiritual" is a biblical concept. If this is how God designed man to nourish himself in the Garden of Eden, in the beginning, then we are to live by the same principle.

You must sow seed for the type of fruit that you desire. In other words, if you want something different, then sow something different. Let me make it simple: get rid of the seeds you've sown if you're not getting the desired results. You've been sowing seeds, but if they are the wrong seeds, then you'll continue getting the wrong fruit. There's a law called, "the law of sowing and reaping." It declares that you will reap what you sow! "Be not deceived; God is not mocked: for whatsoever a man (sows), that shall he also reap" (Galatians 6:7). It's time to make the transition in your mind where you throw away the negative seeds that you've been sowing. Begin to plant the seeds from God's word and you'll get His results for your life. This transition is a part of the process of getting the results that God intended for you.

3 John 1:2 says, "Beloved, I wish above all things that thou (would) prosper and be in (good) health, even as your soul (prospers)." You must get rid of all doubt and negative thinking. You must stand and confess out your mouth what the word of God says. Then, you must believe in your heart that He has already given you promises that He must stand by. Finally, watch God work on your behalf.

In most major cities in world, there are bridges that rise to allow the passage of water vehicles and lower for the passage of land vehicles. Other bridges simply allow land vehicles to pass through. Helping people travel from one side to the other is an important role of bridges. Without bridges, people cannot cross bodies of water. This is how it is in the kingdom of God: transition is the bridge to help you make destiny connections. This may be a hard pill to swallow, but you can make transition your enemy or your friend. If you embrace transition, destiny connections are strategically positioned to assist you in your life in some way.

Destiny connections have exactly what you need in order to fulfill your God-given assignment in the kingdom. Some destiny connections, groomed on the back side of the mountain as Moses was, have been chosen for such a time as this to reveal hidden riches in secret places (Exodus 3:1-6). In order words, they have what you've been praying for. Destiny connections have the knowledge and the connections that will launch and promote your purpose in the kingdom. Please don't allow anyone or anything to stand in your way and keep you from doing what you have to do to crossover in your mind, in your attitude and in your associations to get what God has for you. God is waiting for you to make the transition and crossover by faith in order to be positioned to receive your promises.

We've experienced crying, sadness, and disappointment from hurt and from being let down by people too long. This is the time for us, the body of Christ, to rise in confidence and speak to the mountains of our circumstances and say, "Be gone" and take victory over our enemies. I'm here to declare war against the enemy of our souls and to say to the body of Christ, "Enough is enough, push has come to shove!" Therefore, rise up old sleeping giant; it's time to take the spoils of the land violently for God's glory, to spread the gospel of Jesus Christ to a lost and dying world.

I admit, transition is painful. However, it's necessary for us to pay the price of transitioning in order to get "glory" results that will deliver to this generation the "Wow of God." You may ask, "What's the 'Wow of God'?" It is the overwhelming abundance of God's awesome grace that is displayed by showing off His goodness to a generation that is beyond understanding how or why it happened. The "Wow of God" is the expression of those who benefit from His incredible, phenomenal signs and from the wonders of His riches toward the saints of God.

This generation is about to see something that prevents them from denying that Jesus is Lord. God is about to leave an impression on this generation as it was left on previous generations that experienced a powerful move of God, because these are possibly the last and final generations before the second coming of Christ. I believe that what is about to take place will answer questions, calm fears, remove doubts, settle minds and rekindle Holy Ghost fire within the body of Christ like never before.

Once God takes you through tribulations, then you'll be able to look back to see that "…all things work together for good to them that love God, to them who are the called according to His purpose" (Roman 8:28). You'll be able to say that these tribulations happened because of God's love. Tribulations come to reposition you and you will definitely change once you get through them. Of course, it's hard to see while you're going through them, but you'll see it later.

Don't allow those who are close to you to prevent the necessary "blows" that will accelerate transition in your life. Sometimes, those who are closest to you can become an enemy of change. Although they don't mean any harm, they really can't see, with spiritual eyes, when it comes to you. They see you as someone they love. It's hard sometimes for parents to let go of their children, so that their children can experience life. They try to protect their children from all "blows." By doing so, parents weaken their children to the point where their children won't be able to deal with real life. Hard knocks are good in some cases, because it's the only way you can really learn for yourself. I don't believe that you have to go through everything to learn. But in some cases, it's good, especially in the case of a hard-headed child who won't listen. That child will have to be dealt with by life which is full of trouble. Job 14:1 is a reminder to parents that, "Man that is born of woman is few days, and full of trouble." Some family members and close friends may think that the way God is taking you is not good for you. That's why, sometimes, you can't tell your family everything that God is saying to you about transition, because they may think something is wrong with you. Therefore, you must walk in the knowledge of God's divine process to get to where you're going even if that means transitioning.

Transition frees you from familiar territories, surroundings and schools of thought. Transition could come in the form of one of the many programs out there to help people who need to go through detoxification. People who are hooked on narcotics need some type of support group to assist with their transitioning. This may be good in some cases, but I do believe the power of God in Christ Jesus can set you free from all addictions. There are those, who along with the spiritual transformation, may need a spiritual detoxification type of ministry. The purpose of a spiritual detoxification ministry is to help people to believe differently about themselves. It also encourages people to develop a new way of living to establish a new belief system or school of thought within themselves. This is what God is doing in this hour. He is taking us, the body of Christ, through a school of mental and spiritual transitioning in order to allow us to learn new ways of living through the word of God and the power of God within us.

The more difficult the transition is, the more fruitful you will become if you respond correctly. We must respond correctly, if we're going to reap a great harvest. In nature, what determines a great harvest is in many cases based on what takes place in the ground after the seeds have been planted. Attitude makes a big difference while you're going through any transition.

God requires all of us to have an attitude of appreciation and of thanksgiving. God wants us to praise Him and to give Him thanks in everything, for it's the will of God in

Christ Jesus concerning you and I (1 Thessalonians 5:18). David said, "I will bless the Lord at all times: His praise shall continually be in my mouth" (Psalms 34:1). He wants praise to be in our mouths on a continual basis. We must do it sacrificially, but willingly at the same time. When we give our tithes and offerings, it's sowing seeds. However, in God's eyes, He not only wants us to sow seeds from our substances, but He also is interested in how we sow the seeds. He does not want us to sow seeds grudgingly or out of necessity, because God loves a cheerful giver (2 Corinthians 9:7). Therefore, attitude counts even during difficult transition periods, because God wants to reveal the fruit of His character. The fruit of His character is the fruit of the spirit.

The route to destiny is from glory to glory. You can't go from glory to glory if there's no transition. The assignment of transition is not just to develop your character, but to prepare you for the next dimension of glory. There are different dimensions, higher heights and deeper depths. There are so many avenues and ways that God wants to express His love to and through us, but we must be prepared to be used by God. God wants to reveal Himself greatly through and to us, but we must be ready vessels that can handle that next place in Him. In order to get to the next place in God, we must experience steps toward transition. The steps are from one level of faith to the next level of faith. Your faith will be stretched beyond your imagination, when you accept this "faith walk" (walk in faith). God ordains us to take a "faith walk" in life. When we walk in faith, we will accomplish great things for the expansion of the kingdom.

We need to live by faith and walk by our faiths and not by our sights (Romans 1:17, 2 Corinthians 5:7). This generation is crying for "water walkers", those who dare to trust God and then demonstrate the power of God before the eyes of non-believers. The church must step into realms of faith even though it may be frightening to do so. It's a requirement. In order for the supernatural to enter into the natural, willing vessels must connect, with a singleness of heart, with God to see His wonders unveiled right before our eyes. There's a hunger in the land for God's presence and power to manifest. This generation is desperate for it. Are you willing to be one of those chosen people who will launch out into the deep, let down a net and get the desired results?

There's so much God wants to unfold, but it's going to take people that have "water walking" "mustard seed" faith (Luke 17:6). Dare to believe that you are the one who can be used by God to show Himself mighty in these perilous times.

MY PERSONAL THOUGHTS ON CHAPTER 10

_____

_____

_____

_____

_____

_____

_____

_____

_____

_____

_____

_____

_____

_____

_____

_____

_____

_____

_____

_____

_____

_____

_____

_____

_____

CHAPTER 11

GOD KNOWS HIS PURPOSE IS PAINFUL, BUT PRODUCTIVE

Galatians 6:9; John 15:1-2; Hebrews 12:5-11

God had to allow His own son to feel ignored. It is said that God's ways are past finding out. To fully understand Him is impossible, but worth the search. He will reward those who diligently seek Him (Hebrews 11:6). There's something about the pursuit that brings joy to God, even though He knows that we will never be able to comprehend Him in His fullness. We will never know how God works to bring about His master plan. He uses all things to work together for our good, even though it's not what we ordered or what we would consider something He could use. However, it's not our decision as to how God Himself makes us useful for His divine plans.

He will use anything that brings discomfort to the soul, spirit and body. He uses relationships with people that, at times, will rub you the wrong way, become annoying or just plain irritating. However, the Lord is most concerned about our characters. How we represent the Lord is vital to our "Christian walk." Our approach is important when it comes to how we treat other people.

We have a tendency to be very insensitive when it comes to the hurts and circumstances of others. Ministry should not be presented as though Christianity is not without suffering and tears at times. It cannot be presented as though it's about health and prosperity all the time either. The truth of the matter is that as God's ambassadors, we will not be effective without being touched with the feelings of man's infirmities, sufferings and circumstances. Without compassion, we will not have discernment and we will not utilize our gifts in love. Without feeling the struggles of others, we would be very condemning, self-righteous and pharisaic towards everyone in bad situations. We would find ourselves extremely judgmental and not merciful or sensitive about each other's problems. I have to admit, it's terrible when you have to go through hell just so you can become sympathetic and empathetic towards others. I wish there was another route that we could take in order to walk in humility and meekness. However, the way to the cross is what we all must embrace. The cross of Christ is all about suffering for others.

The song says, "Must Jesus bare the cross alone and all the world go free? Yes, there's a cross for everyone and there's a cross for me." There is definitely a cross for you and me. If we desire to come after the way of Christ, then we must deny ourselves, take up our crosses daily and follow him (Luke 9:23). Notice it says that we are to "take up". We are to pick up our crosses willingly and not with a bad attitude. If you love God, you must suffer some persecution.

Therefore, God allowed His son, Jesus Christ, to be nailed to a cross and to bear the iniquities of us all. He suffered and died for all humanity. What a price just to fulfill a God-given purpose to save us who believe in Jesus Christ as being the son of God! He, willingly, went through all of the agony and shame just to free us from our sin. The judgment of sin had to be paid by someone since man couldn't pay for it. Therefore, God said, "I'll pay for it through my son, Jesus." This is called, "salvation." He purchased our salvation, took our place and became guilty for us. (John 3:16-17)

He didn't sin, but he stood in our place and bore our transgressions. God Himself turned His back on His only begotten son, Jesus, who cried out and said, "My God, My God, why hast thou forsaken me?" (Matthew 27:46) This has always been a puzzling statement for many people, through many generations. God foreknew that He would send His son to be the door or the way for man to escape sin. But in His predestined eternal plan, He ordained this method to bring affliction to the soul and to raise emotions of anguish and turmoil. This says that when we feel affliction, anguish and turmoil that we must depend upon the Father for His strength and deliverance for our survival. It's often been said, "If there's no pain, there's no gain." Grief, which is an emotional turmoil, many times can't be explained. You just simply feel it. You may not be able to express why you feel it, but you feel it. God, somehow and in some way, uses pain as a powerful force. It's like rocket fuel which enables rockets to be launched into space.

God knows that the only way some people will ever move on to the next level in faith and into their God given purposes is through pain. There must be rejections: people must walk away from you. You must deal with the fear of failure. You must go through death-like experiences where the devil paints a picture of nothing but disaster and gloom. You may lose loved ones during this process of preparation. You may have strange experiences such as I had after my third son, who is cognitively impaired, was conceived. It was devastating to find out that there was an issue with our baby in the womb. The baby was growing nicely. In fact, this son was our largest baby. He was ten pounds at birth. After he was born, he was immediately sent to "Special Care." In this specialized unit, the doctors performed several tests. He was then transferred to another hospital for five days. To this day, he has never been diagnosed. We call him our miracle son. He didn't walk until he was five years old. At first the doctors thought he had some kind of syndrome, but this was not the case. I could not understand how God could use me to lay hands on individuals and deaf ears would open, tumors would dissolve and other incurable diseases were healed. Yet, I couldn't and currently can't rebuke the condition that my son still has at 21 years old. However, we believe God for my son's total healing. My father and my sister passed away some years ago. My mother suffers with dementia and other complications that continue to puzzle my mind. Regardless of these things that I just don't understand, the glory of God's presence resides within my ministry.

I believe that after the suffering, comes the glory. He gives us grace or the power and ability to endure hard times. That's how an individual, who may not have a pretty voice, can go to a microphone to sing or speak and the glory of the Lord falls down. His or her pain made him or her powerful. When we allow God to use our situations, then He can be glorified through them and other people are edified through them.

It's not about being comfortable in all situations, but it's all about giving God glory. Sometimes it's difficult to hear, but so much will come out of the sufferings and hard times that you endure. You will produce the fruit of the spirit and reap the blessings of Abraham because you stood and endured with the right perspective while you were going through.

An expensive price tag hangs on a quality product. That's why when you really want to buy something of worth, there are certain stores that are known to sell the best quality materials. There are specific name brand products that are known for their class, because of the quality that goes into their materials and designs. It took time, attention and a process that's above and beyond the norm in order to make an expensive product. Unlike an expensive product, salvation is free. However, the anointing cost something. It cost time, many trials and tribulations, disappointments and mental frustration.

These setbacks, rejections and battles in the mind and in relationships with people are all a part of what I call, "the crushing." Through the crushing, the fragrance within the alabaster box was able to change the fragrance on the outside. Alabaster boxes were used during the Bible days to hold perfumes. Since the alabaster box had to be broken to reach the perfume on the inside, it was only used for important purposes. Just as we would expect today, it isn't good enough to go out and purchase a bottle of perfume and keep the fragrance inside the bottle. We purchase fragrances because we want to make ourselves smell good. Fragrances are intended to bring attention to us. When God breaks us and sends us to the place of crushing, then what He put on the inside of us will flow out from us and change the lives of others. You are more valuable after the crushing is over. God wants us to understand that what He has is in store for us, is far greater than what you and I can ever expect. God said, "If (you) suffer, (you'll) also reign with him…" (2 Timothy 2:12) It's a good thing to know that trouble won't last always and that weeping may endure for the night, but joy is coming in the morning (Psalm 30:5). God's word says "…be not weary in well doing: for in due season, we shall reap, if we faint not" (Galatians 6:9).

That's why Satan doesn't want you to believe that anything good could ever come out of the setbacks you've had in your life. You'd be surprised by those who would benefit from your experiences. What you went through wasn't only for your making and for your benefit, but it was also for the benefit of others. Someone has to be the one to go first in order to make a trail so that there is a pathway for the next generation. People who see and visualize the pathway can walk that walk of faith for their generation so the next generation can do the same. We are more valuable because of the experiences we have under our belts. In many instances, experience is the best teacher, although it is not the only teacher. As previously stated, you really don't have to go through everything if you learn from someone else's experiences. Some things can be learned by listening, if you are not being stubborn or hardheaded.

Don't you wish you could go back in time and do things differently? But if you could, there would be many lessons that you would have never known about life, about yourself and about other people. David said, "It is good for me that I have been afflicted; that I might learn thy statutes" (Psalm 119:71).

MY PERSONAL THOUGHTS ON CHAPTER 11

_____

_____

_____

_____

_____

_____

_____

_____

_____

_____

_____

_____

_____

_____

_____

_____

_____

_____

_____

_____

_____

_____

_____

_____

_____

_____

CHAPTER 12

GOD KNOWS HOW TO PRODUCE POWER

Psalms 43:17; Isaiah 40:31; Isaiah 40:31; Luke 24:49;
Acts 1:8

We must look unto the hills from whence cometh our help, because our help comes from the Lord (Psalm 121:1). We can do all that we can to be better, but we can't be any better than what God made us to be. We need His help. We can try, but there's nothing within our sinfully carnal nature that can assist us in doing better. God orchestrated it so that we can never look to ourselves for help.

Prayer is how we communicate with God. It is a necessity because it aligns the heart with God. Prayer is a method that will get God's attention. There's something about prayer that's reassuring and refreshing. Our Father in heaven designed us to have a spirit and soul within. We came from Him and He knows what will satisfy the spirit and the soul. We won't ever be totally satisfied until we have a relationship with God, the Father, through prayer, and He wants us to give Him complete attention on a daily basis.

God wants us to include Him daily in our decision-making processes. He feels grief when we don't spend time with Him. He wants us to set aside time to spend with Him in prayer and studying His word. He not only wants to hear what we say, but He also wants to talk back to us. God wants an ongoing relationship where He knows that we are comfortable being with him. He knows the heart of man and He knows that all we can give Him is our willingness to come after Him and to serve Him. God chose us - we didn't choose him. It's a pleasure knowing that He created us, allowed us to be born again and permitted His spirit to dwell on the inside of us. What an awesome privilege! So we ought to fight to keep the fellowship that we have with God by not getting off course. This isn't so easy to do. It was through David's brokenness that he said, "Create in me a clean heart, O God; and renew a right spirit within me" (Psalm 51:10) Only God can create a clean heart by His spirit.

It's through Jesus Christ that we can have a pure heart and a right spirit. It's believing in Jesus and in God's word that brings about the cleansing that's needed within. We can't clean ourselves up. It will take His spirit to deliver our spirits. Since He made us, He knows what it will take to get us to line up with His heart.

Endurance through faith, while standing on God's word, eventually brings the glory. It's through waiting on God that patience has her perfect work. The Bible says, "…let patience have her perfect work, that ye may be perfect and entire, wanting nothing" (James 1:4) The time that it takes before God responds is the key to the development of endurance within one's character. It is so important to be able to stick it out when things get tough. Anybody can quit when it gets hard. Yet, God wants us to endure hardness as a good soldier of Jesus Christ (2 Timothy 2:3). He wants us to fight the good fight of faith no matter what. Don't go through life doubting and hopeless, because you might miss an important ingredient that makes you useful for God's glory. That ingredient is faith. Without faith, it's impossible to please God (Hebrews 11:6). Being bitter with a bad attitude doesn't only hurt you, but it ties the hands of God from doing what He does when there's faith and a proper attitude.

We live in a society that wants everything now. No one wants to wait; no one wants to get anything that will cost much effort. People today want things the easy way. Shopping malls are designed in a way which allows us to shop in one location, instead of maneuvering around multiple locations to get what we want. Shopping online is the thing now, because through technology, you don't have to leave the comfort of your home while you are purchasing products from all over the world. There are instant coffee makers, microwaves, iPods, iPads and cells phones for the "I need it NOW" generation. In fact, cell phones are so elaborate that they can serve all types of quick communication purposes. Therefore, it's quite challenging as believers in Jesus Christ to understand what God means by waiting and enduring. Our children live in a society that feels that it's not necessary to finish school and to get a good education, especially when they can make a whole lot of money selling drugs and doing damnable things in the world. The concept of waiting and enduring just doesn't fit our culture.

I'd rather wait on God and develop stamina and stability through trusting in Him than getting instant success without wisdom, knowledge and understanding. Endurance is an awesome quality to have because it says that you can take what life dishes out and yet make it. Wow! That's powerful in itself: we have the ability within us not to quit or give up. Endurance gives you spiritual power and mental strength while building character at the same time. Frustration will definitely come as you are developing spiritually, because it takes time to learn what life as a Christian is all about.

I remember having many frustrating moments when I wondered how long it would take before God came through for me in terms of finding a location for our church. After we had outgrown our church in Maywood, Illinois we needed to rent a high school auditorium for nine years. We would frequently receive calls or get a tip that a particular parcel of land was available. There must have been at least twelve to fourteen different pieces of property that our leadership actually looked at. Excitement would temporarily enter our lives and then with disappointment after disappointment, the excitement would dissipate. There were times when I was at the church late at night and early in the morning praying for a breakthrough. I fasted day and night while I was waiting. We held many shut-ins where I stayed up all night at the church, but I waited. Waiting was a part of my life. As all this was going on, God was working on my character. I couldn't see it at the time, but God had to remove some stuff out of me so He could prepare me for what He had for me and where He was taking me. God is so good. He finally came through for me and our patient and supportive congregation because we continued looking and waiting on God. The word of God says, "...let us not be weary in well doing: for in due season we shall reap, if we faint not" (Galatians 6:9). I felt like fainting at times, because it was not easy. I had to overcome my own fears. However, God, who is merciful and kind, sustained me. I got stronger and wiser while traveling on my journey.

We acquired the property in February of 2002. On July 7, 2002, we marched into our new facility. It was the former Loewe's theatre which had six theatres. We transformed two of the larger theatres into sanctuaries. We are confident that He which has begun a good work shall perform it until the day of Jesus Christ (Philippians 1:6).

To God be the glory for the things He has done!

MY PERSONAL THOUGHTS ON CHAPTER 12

_____

_____

_____

_____

_____

_____

_____

_____

_____

_____

_____

_____

_____

_____

_____

_____

_____

_____

_____

_____

_____

_____

_____

_____

III. THE MODEL OF MERCY

CHAPTER 13

GOD'S POSITIONING IS FOR PROMISE AND PERMANENT FULFILLMENT

Genesis 12: 1-3; Joshua 23:1-5

What do you do when it doesn't look the way God said it would be? I heard many prophesies concerning my destiny and how God was going to give me a worldwide ministry, prior to my son Terrell's birth. Terrell is my youngest son and the child I mentioned earlier. Prophet after Prophet came and spoke powerful words into my life.

Then, my wife kept getting prophesies about becoming a millionaire. I began wondering why no one ever prophesized to me about my being a millionaire, too. However, I would say, "Well, I'm her husband, and if she comes into the wealth first, then I'll be wealthy as well."

When my wife was pregnant with Terrell(our third son), a prophet came and told her that there was some type of complication, but gave us hope concerning Terrell. So, we went to the doctor for a checkup. We found out that Terrell might have some type of syndrome that they had not detected. The doctor put my wife and I in a bad position: the doctor wanted us to decide whether we would get rid of the child or raise him with the deficiency. Of course, we chose to raise him and we've been blessed to have wonderful caregivers to help assist us with caring for Terrell. We knew that God had ordained us, because we had to fulfill an assignment in our lives that we couldn't figure out. We just had to trust God. We had to accept the fact that God chose us to be Terrell's parents, no matter how it appeared to others. We are "special parents" for a special needs son. It's easy to move on with your life when there's no limp or when there's nothing that you or anyone else can do that could slow you down. But, living with circumstances and challenges that are mentally attached to you, that you cannot ignore because they are a part of you, is not easy.

What's so amazing about God is that He gives you grace to handle what life brings. Life reminds me of a woman's womb. When a woman becomes pregnant, she does not know the sex of the child or what the child is like until it's born. After the birth, she can hold her baby and look closely into the face of her baby. She can play with her baby and watch her baby smile, laugh and cry. None of this can happen until the baby is born. Life is the same way. We have to take life one day at a time to experience the actual outcome.

With all that has happened in my life, you would think that God would change His mind concerning the call upon my life, but He did not. He already knew about the challenges that I would have. He foreknew and predestined my way.

Therefore, I have learned how to trust Him even when things look different, difficult and distorted.

We will go through tests and even chastising by God when needed. However, what's meant for us, we'll get. God is not into playing games. He is about producing for the gain of the kingdom. It's the Father's good pleasure to give you the kingdom (Luke 12:32). So remember that God is positioning you for the promise for permanent fulfillment. The "Promised Land" was given to Abraham and to his descendants. No matter how long it took, God said that it was theirs. It's important to know that God keeps His promises. He's not a man that He should lie, nor the son of man that He should repent. If He said it, He will surely bring it to pass (Numbers 23:19).

The wilderness is only a means to get you to your promise. The journey that we must all face will, at times, appears disheartening. If we had a road map which gave detailed directions of the exact way to get to our destinations in life, then life would be so much easier. It's not so because life has unexpected turns, dips, twirls, lifts, pulls and drops. We feel discouraged, at times, because we don't like unexpected turns, etc. They take our minds and hearts into directions different from those in which we started out. Dips may cause imbalances in our lives. A dip may also cause a delay in our lives in order to get our equilibrium back, so we can get back on track. Then, here comes something else that hits us so hard that we get twirled around in life. We are left confused and dizzy, not knowing which way to go. Sometimes, God sends a lift or an oasis in the desert and often you will find out that the lift or the oasis was just to give you a temporary break. On some occasions, pulls from within your mind try to persuade you not to trust God. If you're not in "right" relationship with God, you will think for a moment that God does not like you because He allowed things to take place in your life. God's chosen people, the children of Israel, were discouraged because of the "way." Scripture tells us that it was the "way" that God chose for them to take.

Job said, "...he (knows) the way that I take: when he hath tried me, I shall come forth as gold" (Job 23:10). Job's story was not a good one at the beginning. Only the first few verses of chapter one tell us how blessed Job was. Then life turned for Job. There are forty-two chapters of his story that show how difficult and challenging life was for Job. The last few verses of chapter forty-two talk about how God turned things around for Job and how Job ended up more blessed than he was in the beginning.

David said, "Yea, though I walk through the valley of the shadow of death, I will fear no evil: for thou art with me..." (Psalm 23:4). When walk through the "valley of the shadow of death," we are supposed to walk through, not die there. We are not to stay in fear. We are to live by faith, for the just shall live by faith (Romans 1:17). Although fear torments us, we must learn how to not live life afraid while we're living by faith. Fear is an emotion and we must learn how to face our fears, starve our doubts and feed our faith.

Some of you might look back and wonder why it is taking you so long to move ahead in life. One of the reasons might be that you are having a difficult time accepting the fact that you feel and sense two different things going on within you. First, you must deal with the emotions that come from past experiences. Like physical scars, scars of the soul leave marks on your mind. Each time you think about what happened to you, you begin to feel grief or sadness and it drains you and takes away your drive. Second, you just can't help seeing what you see about your future. You are a visionary with great thoughts about your future, your "expected end." You have two things battling against each other in your mind. If you give into the first scenario, dealing with the emotions from your past, then you'll live life stuck in the past. If you give into the second scenario, the life of the visionary, then you will keep the drive to birth what you see.

Always remember that those who see a promising vision cannot help but to feel motivated and inspired to make it happen. Visionaries can't afford to fulfill their God given visions based on how they feel. A visionary must learn to ignore his or her feelings and to focus on outcomes. Visionaries can't allow their feelings or thoughts to slow them down or to their stop progress. Feelings are dangerous, because they constantly change. Never build your life on how you feel or make important decisions on how you feel unless it's God given feelings or knowledge within you.

There's also a danger in staying in the wrong place too long and not overcoming sins and weights. Time goes by and before you know it, it's gone. Time has an assignment, and you and I have an appointment with time. Time is never to be looked at wastefully; it's to be taken seriously. God made time for man to accomplish and to fulfill his purpose while he is on the earth.

When a person does not utilize the time God has allotted, then he or she loses focus and follows his or her emotions. Some people live life bitter because they live in regret. They are sorry they didn't go back to school to get a better education, sad that they made bad choices in life or they are depressed that they are stuck with children from men who aren't their husbands or women who aren't their wives. They are emotionally drained over the debt that they have to live with and they feel sorry because of what they did.

If you have to ask someone to stay on you and to help get you moving, please do it. Life is too short for you to get stuck and not leave anything of any worth for your family and for your children. You want to leave something that you can be proud of, something that will be a blessing not only to you and your family, but also to God. God finds pleasure in the prosperity of His people. I told you that it's the Father's good pleasure to give you the kingdom. Whatever you do, keep walking through the "valley of the shadow of death" because there's light at the end of the tunnel, if you keep your eyes on Jesus. He will bring you out.

Some people will never reach their goals and dreams because of their mind-sets and their unbelief. That statement almost brings tears to my eyes. If I really focus on the truth of the matter, it's very sad and extremely devastating to even think that I would not be able to see the manifestation of God's promises in my life. I would hate to believe that those who are reading this book would finish it only to say it's a good book and not do something to enhance or change their lives. Don't be like the scripture in the Bible that speaks about always learning but never coming into the knowledge of the truth (2 Timothy 3:7). Don't be a hearer only, but be a doer of the word. We are required to hear the word of God to gain faith, because faith cometh by hearing and hearing by the word of God (Romans 10:17). It's most essential that you are in a church that preaches the word of God, because you can't afford to be anywhere where you cannot grow in faith. If you don't develop in faith, then you won't trust God and you won't step out on His word to claim all the promises that God has for you.

It's the Father's good pleasure to bless us. God really wants to see us have all that He has for us. He wants us to prosper and to be in health even as our souls prosper (3 John 1:2). According to Matthew 6:33, "But seek ye first the kingdom of God, and his righteousness; and all these things shall be added unto you." This sounds like a father who's very interested in the success of his children and wants the best for them in life. John 10:10 reminds us that Jesus came so that we might an abundant life or a full life "…I am come that they might have life, and that they might have it more abundantly." An interpretation of more abundantly could be, "to the fullest or to overflowing." God gave benefits to his children who are in Christ Jesus. We are the seed of Abraham, and it's our covenant right to be heirs of God and joint-heirs as His adopted children. Adopted children are included in the benefit plan. He forgives us of all our iniquities. He heals all of our diseases. He redeems us from destruction. He crowns us with love, kindness and tender mercies and He satisfies our mouths with good things (Psalm 103:5). We have a father who wanted to show how much He loves us by sending His only begotten to son to this earth to die for us in order to give us an inheritance amongst those who are sanctified.

You are born to possess the promise; to fulfill God given dreams and aspirations. No longer allow set-backs to come back in your face. You must declare, "That was then, but this is now!" Each day is a new day - a day that the Lord has made. We are to rejoice and be glad in it. Wake up daily saying, "God is going to do something special with my life today." Wake up thinking it, saying it and believing it!

Do not allow anything to stop you from being an achiever in life. Make bold statements, "I will never again live life limited." You have a father who is so big that He can do anything. He can take you anywhere and will help you to accomplish whatever He tells you to accomplish. You should live life with great expectancy. This doesn't negate the fact that you will need to deal with problems. Yet, we should not go through life anticipating the next problem to arise. If it comes, it just comes. You need to have a different attitude and perspective about trouble. If you don't get a handle on trouble, then trouble will definitely handle you. This means that when it comes, you must deal with it accordingly and keep on moving forward. The only way you can accept this theory about life is by having the power of God in Christ Jesus dwelling in your heart. He's made you the head and not the tail. The head includes those who are possessors and have made up their minds that they will refuse to give up and give in to what troubles bring.

I refuse to be bitter and so I made up my mind to be better. When God told Abraham to go into a land that He would show him, He meant that the land was not a hoax. It was a true location and territory where people could actually live. Joshua and Caleb saw it years before it was actually obtained. God allowed twelve men, who represented the twelve tribes of Israel, to see the Promised Land. They stayed forty days and saw grapes and fruit that were huge and luscious. However, they also saw giants in the land. Seeing giants brought great fear to ten of these men. They came back reporting that they were as grasshoppers compared to the giants. Do you see? They stated out of their hearts how they viewed themselves versus what God had said about them having the land that was promised. If they'd thought about it, they would have had a different report, but what was in their hearts came out of their mouths. This is a lesson that we need to learn from the Israelites. Out of their mouths, they spoke damnation and destruction to their own destinies and this is the reason why the Israelites did not enter the promise land. Those men made God angry and as a result, they died because of their unbelief while walking through the wilderness.

The unbelief amongst the ten leaders of the Israelites affected the whole nation of Israel because of their words. There were only two Israeli leaders who believed God and walked in faith. They were Caleb and Joshua. Caleb said that they could go at once to possess the land for "we are well able to overcome it" (Numbers 13:30). The report I want you to have is that you are well able to accomplish your dreams and goals.

There will be giants that will face you and come across your path while you are traveling towards destiny, but you must have faith in God's ability to make things happen for you as He has told you.

MY PERSONAL THOUGHTS ON CHAPTER 13

_____

_____

_____

_____

_____

_____

_____

_____

_____

_____

_____

_____

_____

_____

_____

_____

_____

_____

_____

_____

_____

CHAPTER 14

GOD NEVER INTENDED TO SATISFY YOU TEMPORARILY, HIS PLAN IS TO MAKE YOU LIE DOWN IN GREEN PASTURES.

Psalms 23:2; Deuteronomy 28:1-14

It is the Lord's will to bless us naturally and spiritually. Deuteronomy 28 speaks about God's promised blessings. It states very clearly that God always intended for His children to walk as the head and not as the tail. God wants us to be blessed in all that we do because we represent Him, we are an extension of Him, we are His children and we are sons of God. We are kings, and ambassadors of Jesus Christ. We represent the kingdom of God on the earth and He satisfies us with long life and pleasures for evermore (Psalm 91:16/Psalm 16:11).

God's word should never be taken lightly. Through His word, He is trying to give the body of Christ the knowledge of His ways, how he thinks and how He operates. It is so important that we learn kingdom principles for ourselves because we benefit tremendously from them. God's will is that we live long, pleasurable lives, but "religious systems" keep us limited and frustrated. Religious systems cause people to feel that the more "broke" they are financially, the more grounded they are in God. The less they have, the more they're separating themselves from this world.

Individuals who are caught in a religious system that condemns people for wanting to live above poverty are denying themselves kingdom principles. The "poor and happily broke mentality" actually separates us from God, and that is not what He intended or how He operates.

There are blessings that have been stored up for the righteous man, woman, boy or girl. In other words, the blessings accumulate over time. We have been given the ability, by God, to live life according to the power that's in us. What God gave us in Christ Jesus is more powerful than we'll ever know. Ephesians 3:20 confirms the power that works in us, "Now unto him that is able to do exceeding abundantly above all that we ask or think, according to the power that (works) in us." As long as we're in this body, we're entitled to all that God has for us in Christ. However, we are hindered by our finite minds. God is infinite in all He does. If you ever tap into the revelation of who Jesus is, and who you are in Christ Jesus, you will be able to accomplish great things for God.

Religious systems do not want us to appear exalted, but humbled by every truth in God's word. This conflicts with kingdom principles because the word of God tells us that we have authority as believers. I understand that non-believers do not want believers to walk around thinking that they are superior. However, we, as believers, are only who we are because of Christ.

For many years, the church has been in a position of learning. God has been teaching the body of Christ that it's never been about our righteousness or our works; it has always been Christ's working, developing and strengthening us as believers. This truth can be sobering. We have to accept the fact that if Christ doesn't do the work in and through our lives to help others, then we will never be in a place to produce the power that God intended for us.

In rough times, it's sometimes challenging to comprehend spiritual matters. If you understand that God wants to have full control of your thoughts and the way you think, you also acknowledge that He can help you with all of your struggles. Your thought life (your thoughts and the way you think) determines your progress. Philippians 2:5 affirms that we should, "Let this mind be in (us), which was also in Christ Jesus..." God wants us to change the way we think, so He can teach us the operations of His kingdom. God's thoughts are not our thoughts and our ways are not His ways. According to the Prophet Isaiah, "For as the heavens are higher than the earth, so are (God's) ways higher than (our) ways, and (God's) thoughts than (our) thoughts" (Isaiah 55:8-9). We can't always understand God's ways, but we must walk by faith and not by sight in rough times. God doesn't need the economy to change before He blesses His people. Faith moves God to activate the process that's needed for the believer to experience the blessings that are assigned to his or her life.

Remember; God took nothing, but made everything. Please keep that in mind! He's not moved by our lack, but by our faith. He provided for His people during previous economic crises. He will certainly do it again, because He will never forsake His people. He will never break His covenant, no matter what. So, this is a great time for God to show His goodness and come through for his people. God is glorified even more when it appears that we don't have anything to work with. God is preparing a table before us in the presence of our enemies. David said, "The Lord is my shepherd; I shall not want" (Psalm 23:1). If He's your shepherd, you don't have to live in poverty. You may go through the valley of the shadow of death, but you don't have to fear evil for God is with you. You must come to the place where you can say to yourself, "Even though I don't know what to do, all is well."

You must take courage as the woman in 2 Kings 4:8-37 did. The Prophet Elisha told the woman that she would "embrace a son" and the woman conceived. When the woman's son grew up, he died in her arms. After her son's death she said, "It shall be well." Regardless of her circumstances, she believed God. The woman told her servant to, "Drive, and go forward; slack not thy riding for me, except I bid thee." She was on a mission to meet the Prophet Elisha, the man of God who spoke God's blessings into her life regarding her son. Her feeling was that if he spoke God's blessings before, then when she saw the prophet, he would speak God's blessings again. God performed a miracle when she went to see the prophet. The dead man got up and he lived. She could have given up and said, "Oh, well, what's the use? Yes, he was born, but he's dead now. Well, God did give me a son, but it's all over now." But no, this woman refused to accept a short life-span for her son. She held on to her faith and kept on riding to where the man of God was. In these times, you've got to have the drive to live, and let nothing and no one hinder your progress.

In our lack of understanding, we try to bless ourselves, but it doesn't work. Please don't get me wrong, there is a biblical principle that we all must honor. If we don't work, then we don't eat! 2 Thessalonians 3:10 says "...if any would not work, neither should he eat." Thus, the principle is faith without works is dead or if you do not perform some action, then you will get no results. So, I know that God wants us to participate in networking and establishing divine connections. This is important in obtaining our destinies. No one gets there alone; it takes others to assist us in the process. Sometimes we include others, but we don't include God while pursuing His best for us.

When we don't acknowledge God as the director of our paths, we make moves and decisions that we wish we didn't make. Instead of asking for God's guidance in the beginning, we ask God's help at the end. We end up hooking up with people that detour us from where we're suppose to go, because we feel it's the right thing to do at that time. "Except the Lord build the house, they labor in vain that build it: exccpt the Lord keep the city, the watchman waketh but in vain" (Psalm 127:1). So let God build your life, your marriage, your family, your ministry and your business.

MY PERSONAL THOUGHTS ON CHAPTER 14

_____

_____

_____

_____

_____

_____

_____

_____

_____

_____

_____

_____

_____

_____

CHAPTER 15

GOD'S PLAN IS TO TAKE YOU ON A FAR JOURNEY TO SEE AND EXPERIENCE HIS GOODNESS.

1 Corinthians 2:9; Ephesians 3:20

You can't even imagine what God has in store for you. It's beyond what you can ask. Picture yourself going up in an airplane. After getting up in the air, you look out the window in amazement at the beauty and wonders of God's creation. While on the ground, you could never imagine by looking up what it's like up above the clouds. You have to get up there to really experience it. There is so much that God wants to show us on this journey of faith.

It has taken the body of Christ decades to come to the revelation of the authority God has given us through His son, Jesus Christ. In the past, we've worked hard trying to receive what's already been given to us. Remember what Hosea, the Prophet said, "My people are destroyed for lack of knowledge..." (Hosea 4:6). Many God fearing believers have gone on to be with the Lord, who didn't have to go so soon. However, because of their lack of knowledge concerning their health, they could not deal with the cares of this life. Living in fear and stress affected them physically and caused them to have early deaths. I refuse to live life from day to day proclaiming that God, the father of the universe, is my father, and yet live beneath my privilege. I know too much of the Bible, and too many stories of great patriarchs who obeyed God and how He came through for them. Jesus is the same yesterday, today and forever (Hebrews 13:8). Therefore, if He did it then, He can and will do it now.

I found out for myself that we must first allow God to work on our minds and how we think. Thoughts are pictures painted within the imagination of man. Thoughts are ideas and ideas, whether good or bad, are like seeds. If you plant a seed, then the seed will do what it's designed to do and that is to grow. Therefore, whatever thoughts are planted in your mind, will grow. God clearly knows that. That's why we must be careful what we allow to enter into our thoughts. We must be doorkeepers of our hearts and minds. We must allow the Holy Spirit to check us daily as well as throughout the day.

We do not have time to allow filthy information to filter in and out of our minds. It's unfruitful and unproductive. If gossip, lies, and other filthy information enter into our thoughts, then someone will eventually get hurt. That someone might be you. God's word tells us that we are to have the mind of Christ. Having the mind of Christ is not just a good idea; it's a statement of position and possession. As children of God and believers in Christ Jesus, we have the mind of Christ even if unholy thoughts periodically enter our minds. When unholy thoughts come into our minds, we must proclaim God's word and stand on His word until our thoughts begin to change. Since we already have the mind of Christ, we must work out our own soul's salvation with fear and trembling. In other words, we have to allow the principles of God's word to be applied through meditation and study day and night. This enables us to become transformed by the renewing of our minds (Romans 12:2).

We also must change how we speak. When our minds go through a cleansing process and our spirits are convicted by the Holy Spirit and God's word, then we will start to notice that we need to speak differently. God will help us to recognize when the things we say are not pleasing to Him. Eventually, when we say things that are not pleasing to God, those things will start to bother us. I don't think that we can continue to have a relationship with God and say words that are inappropriate for Christians to say. I believe that we cannot use words that do not reflect Christian conduct. The Holy Spirit will deal with our hearts and show us what pleases God and what does not please God. The Bible contains many scriptures that shed light on what we should say and how we should say it. For example, we can't say words that will bring harm to others. The Holy Spirit is pure and righteous, and will not dwell inside of us while we are hurting people. As a result, we must be careful how we speak to one another and what we say to one another. Sometimes, speaking inappropriately will really irritate your soul. Irritation often comes when God is working His divine purpose within our hearts and within our characters. God operates by principles and He wants to bless us above our imaginations. What we say could hinder God's process of becoming all that He can be in our lives. "Out of the heart, the mouth speaks" is a profound truth.

There are natural and spiritual laws set in the universe by God. The law of gravity is a natural law. Basically, it was created to hold things down on earth. When things go up, gravity invariably pulls them back down to earth. The laws set by God to govern that which is spiritual are spiritual laws. Spiritual laws are revealed by God through His word. Proverbs 18:21 says, "Death and life are in the power of the tongue: and they that love it shall eat the fruit thereof." Spiritual laws give the human tongue authority to speak life or death. The awesome authority God gave the human tongue comes with tremendous responsibility. First, we must be aware of what we say because people could be wounded by what we say. Second, if we don't say the right things, then things just won't work for us, even if we say we have faith and we believe we are doing everything God told us to do. We need to say the right things at the right time to the right people.

Destruction has taken place in the lives of God's people, not through God's fault, His design or His will for it to be. Some things occur because of our free will to choose our own outcomes. We can decide how we want to live this life. We can do what we want to do and say what we want to say, but nothing will ever change if we settle for what we've already received. Changing how we speak is a requirement for those of us who want more of God and more from God. We must possess control or temperance, which is a fruit of the spirit. We already have it within us, we just have to work the principles of self-discipline in order for the fruit of temperance to be recognized in what we say and do. If we practice watching over our words, then we will not allow others to get us caught up in messy conversations that are not only damaging to the characters of others, but are damaging to our characters as well. On the surface, messy conversations appear harmless but they cause cancer in the spirit.

Someone who keeps downing people and talking about others unconsciously develops a bad attitude and a poor disposition. No one feels comfortable speaking to a person with a bad attitude and a poor disposition about private matters, because it's already known that the outcome is going to be negative. How fruitful or edifying is it to be perceived by others as the person who never hears the truth about himself/herself? How fruitful is it to never admit that you have a problem with gossip or slander? Members of the body of Christ are damaged in many instances because of what people have said about them. As a result, churches have split, families have been destroyed and relationships have been ended. There is nothing left to show from broken relationships and damaging words but a trail of blood that says to the next generation, "This is what happens when we don't use our tongues to speak words of comfort, to offer encouragement and to impart edification." Even when we must provide correction, our words should correct and not kill. If utilized appropriately, not in judgment or condemnation, the tongue builds up and edifies others. Therefore, our tongues must be governed by the Holy Spirit, God's word and self discipline.

We can't help but to hear bad news at times. However, we must be strong enough to know what we should prevent from settling in the fertile ground of our minds. We must be determined to think on pure and lovely things. These days, it seems like nothing is lovely; it looks like everything is horrible. Making a conscious effort to think on wonderful, beautiful things will bring a smile to the face and a lift to the heart. Also, we must search for positive reports. We hear bad news all of the time: we hear it in our homes, on our jobs, in and about schools and in the media. When reading the newspaper, we receive negative news concerning our cities, our states and our nations. We have an ongoing fight to stay positive because God wants us to think on good things. Philippians 4:8 speaks to us about our thoughts, "Finally, brethren, whatsoever things are true, whatsoever things are honest, whatsoever things are just, whatsoever things are pure, whatsoever things are lovely, whatsoever things are of good report; if there be any virtue, and if there be any praise, think on these things."

We develop and strengthen our abilities to avoid weaknesses when we fight for what's good and when we refuse to settle for what's evil or negative. Since we have the mind of Christ, we must keep our mental guards up and not let them down, no matter what happens. We must also make up our minds that we are going to "jump in and go all the way", knowing that it's a fight to the finish. In order to fight to the finish, we have to have the faith to act on God's word.

Staying where we are in life means we don't need faith, because it does not take any faith to reject God's word or His help. If we are going to live life desiring peace, harmony and success, we need faith and divine help. It doesn't make sense to try to attain peace, harmony or success by human efforts alone because the power of God moves us along on our journeys and on our "walks of faith." However, we must leave shallow waters and launch out into the deep in our faiths. We must ask ourselves: "How far do we really want to go?" and "How far in this walk of faith do we really want to go to get there?"

Some believers are satisfied with being saved and helping others to come to know Jesus Christ as their personal savior. This is absolutely awesome that people have the heart and goals to be saved and to help others come to salvation. All believers should aspire salvation and to present salvation to others because of their love for God.

As we grow and mature in our walk with God and study His word, we learn more about the new covenant that He made with us in mind. This covenant severs the generational curse related to the original sin of Adam, and establishes new things for the believer in Jesus Christ. Jesus Christ came that we might have life outside of the curse of Adam and a life that is abundant (John 10:10). Galatians 3:29 tells the believer that, "…if ye be Christ's, then are ye Abraham's seed, and heirs according to the promise." Since we are the seed of Abraham, we are redeemed from "under the law, that we might receive the adoption of sons" (Galatians 4:5). The Bible says, "And if children, then heirs; heirs of God, and joint-heirs with Christ…" (Romans 8:17). Therefore, we have an ability to do more, to achieve more and we are favored more than non-believers because we are His righteous seed – we are his children.

We need to let God really bless us the way He knows how to. Only God truly knows how to bless us and when to bless us. If we work the principles of God's word and wait for Him patiently and diligently, then He will come through. I've always believed that God is not a respecter of persons, but He respects His principles. In Romans 2:11 the Apostle states that, "…there is not respect of persons with God." He watches those who have faith and He knows those who do not have faith. That's why the Bible says in

Luke 12:32 "Fear not, little flock; for it is your Father's good pleasure to give you the kingdom." God knows that fear torments us and keeps us from receiving benefits. In many instances, we allow fear to prevent us from stepping out and taking risks. Moving out in faith to get what the Father has prepared for us can be risky, but it's His good pleasure to give to us His kingdom. He wants to share kingdom results with us.

God wants us to experience a life of kingdom manifestation. This means that He wants to show us, when we permit Him to rule and govern our lives, that we can have whatsoever we say according to His will. Then, we can experience the abundant life in Christ Jesus. Job said, "...he (knows) the way that I take: when he (has) tried me, I (will) come forth as gold." God's intention is for an expensive product to come out of the fire of life. God knows how to bless us and how to prepare us to be blessed. It is through the fiery trials of life that we get ready for greater manifestations of His blessings. God's goodness is not based upon our desire for His blessings; God is good because He wants to be good.

One of the shortest verses in the bible is "He that loveth not knoweth not God; for God is Love" (1 John 4:8). God is made up of love. He is the pure essence of love. He does not view humanity through anger, but through love. John 3:16 reminds us, "For God so loved the world, that he gave his only begotten Son, that whosoever believeth in him should not perish, but have everlasting life." He loves us, just because! Wow! What an answer! What a reason! Even while we were yet sinners, Jesus died for us! "But God commendeth his love toward us, in that, while we were yet sinners, Christ died for us" (Romans 5:8). He took care of the issue of sin before we were even born.

God loved the fellowship, intimacy and relationship He had in the garden with Adam. Each day God would spend time talking with Adam. After Adam sinned, God couldn't have fellowship, intimacy or relationship with him because God is a Holy God. The issue of sin had to be dealt with. That's why God sent His son Jesus, who was sinless, to put on all of our sins and to become the ultimate sin offering for us. He was judged for our sins so we could be free and so God could once again have fellowship, intimacy and relationship with humankind. The blood of Jesus served as our atonement and gave us redemption. God was no longer angry because of Jesus.

God put Adam and Eve out of the garden, but He won't have to put us out of the secure place of promise, because provision was made for us to have access to the promises of God through Christ Jesus. However, if we choose to walk in total disobedience to God's new covenant, then we won't have access to the door of mercy that is given to all who believe in Christ Jesus. "The Lord is not slack concerning his promise, as some men count slackness; but is longsuffering to us-ward, not willing that any should perish, but that all should come to repentance" (2 Peter 3:9). So, it's really up to us if we want to experience limited blessings or unlimited blessings. He wants to reveal His goodness, but only to those who are qualified and have a heart for God and for people.

MY PERSONAL THOUGHTS ON CHAPTER 15

_____

_____

_____

_____

_____

_____

_____

_____

_____

_____

_____

_____

_____

_____

_____

_____

Chapter 16

God revives and restores

Psalms 85:1-13; Psalms 138:7; Isaiah 57:15; Hosea 14:1-8;
Joel 2:25-27; Nehemiah chapters 1 – 6

"The Lord redeems the life of his servants; none of those who take refuge in him will be condemned" (Psalm 34:22). Your time is in God's hands and it is the heart of God that will make you whole. "Being whole" means to be entire, full and complete. I don't know many people who feel whole and satisfied with their lives. Most people are not fulfilled or do not feel complete. They are simply satisfied with life or with all the wonderful experiences life has given them. Even though I have called some aspects of life "The American Dream," I know it's not really the case. There's nothing about the reality of life that gives you everything you want and desire.

Sometimes there are wet pillows that are soaked from nightly displays of anguish and disappointment. Shedding tears over past events and heartache can be even more stressful when you know that crying doesn't really remove the memories. If anything, prolonged crying makes you feel worse. Crying can be good, for a brief period of time, since it's an emotional expression that brings a sense of relief for the moment. However, if it's done too long, then it's not healthy. It can take you into depression and into a deeper sense of regret and misery. For some, it's difficult to tell how much heartache they've experienced because they have become skilled at hiding their feelings. To sum it up, regardless of how you express heartache, heartache can become a roadblock or a stepping stone to your destiny.

God wants to make you whole, but if you are tied to your pain, then your pain may bring you temporary pleasure from your past. This is not the correct way to view emotional trauma, but the mind is addictively satisfied in deception. Living with deception causes the loss of time, sapped energy, and a hopeless heart. No wonder some people commit suicide over the "ghost stuff." I say the "ghost stuff," because no one can see what you're fighting. If someone were to watch you up close, he or she would wonder who you were talking to, because it would appear as if there was a ghost in your house or someone sitting next to you talking to you. As Christians, we definitely don't believe in ghosts; however, when you are fighting the unseen, it appears that something is tormenting you behind the scenes of life where no one else can see. You're living with company that you hate. You want to put them out of your house, but you don't know how, because they've become so comfortable now and it's hard to get rid of them. The ghost is the enemy of your destiny. It's your inner enemy called "the devil." He's a roaring lion, seeking whom he may devour (1 Peter 5:8). He roars in your mind and no one can hear him but you. He makes lots of noise trying to detour you from hearing the voice of the Lord.

Satan's voice is not designed to comfort or encourage, but to destroy. If you're ever going to become whole, you have to have another companion. That companion is Jesus Christ. He alone will make you whole. The Bible says, "The thief (comes) not, but for to steal, and to kill, and to destroy: I am come that they may have life, and that they might have it more abundantly" (John 10:10). The challenge is to get over what you've lost, so you can recover.

I've watched the 400 Meter Hurdles event during the Olympic Games and during track and field meets on television. As the runners ran, I saw that the challenge was to gain speed and to maintain technique. It appeared extremely difficult to me because as they were running they had to raise their legs high enough to get over each hurdle, one at a time. Each contestant had to be in great shape in order to keep the required pace while maneuvering over each hurdle without getting tired. This is a life lesson. When hurdles come in your life, you are not expected to jump over every hurdle at the same time. You just need to be ready to jump over hurdles as they come. I also learned that athletes who jump hurdles must train to run fast and to jump high. This is another life lesson. If you are going to achieve in life and become your best, you must prepare to run faster and to jump higher than you ever have. This means that you must be able to move quickly and in the timing of God. When the door opens, face your opposition and use your God-given faith like never before to launch out into the deep. Leap higher in faith to reap the harvest that God has already prepared for you even if you don't win every race.

You must get beyond living life in a dazed state because you have regrets. At times you've sought things that you didn't achieve, and you were left in a daze or stunned by why things didn't happen for you. You may have desired a new home, a mate and/or money and when you didn't get what you wanted, you were shocked that it didn't happen for you. You might have even been speechless. Eventually, all you saw was what should have happened, and what could have happened. It had you stuck. You began staring at the wrong thing. That thing is called "regret." Regret sets up residence and leaves you dazed after you experience many disappointments and perceived failures. You must get beyond past disappointments and perceived failures because the memory of them will become your enemy.

Shake yourself, get over it and live again. There's life after a rip! Have you ever purchased an expensive outfit that you loved only to find out that there was a flaw or a small tear in it? It was reduced in value because it was flawed. Don't allow your flaws to make you feel that you're not a quality person with self-worth. You are God's choice and He wants to use your life, even though you are flawed or damaged in some areas. Don't give up on yourself, because you are special and you have God's name-brand upon your life.

"And God said, 'Let us make man in our own image, after our likeness: and let them have dominion over the fish of the sea, and over the fowl of the air, and over the cattle, and over all the earth, and over every creeping thing that (creeps) upon the earth'" (Genesis 1:26).

If you are born again, then you are God's child and no matter what's happened that has left you flawed, you can get over it and live again. It may seem like it's taking a long time for you to recover, but you have to allow recovery to take place and live again. Even though people may see your flaws, don't stop living. As long as you have breath in your body, you have life. Some seamstresses have to repair rips that are very difficult to repair. But a great seamstress can repair a torn area and make it look as though it had never been damaged. That's what God will do for your life. He will mend your broken-heart, lift up your hung-down head and repair your rip so it looks as though it had never been damaged.

God is in charge of time. Only He can make up lost time and give you double for your trouble. Isaiah 61:7 confirms this because the Prophet told the people, "For your shame ye shall have double; and for confusion they shall rejoice in their portion: therefore in their land they shall possess the double: everlasting joy shall be unto them." Have you ever told someone that you'd make something up to them and their patience made you want to go out of your way to do even more than what you were intending to do? That's the way God is - He will give you more than what you ever expected from Him. He will make up for lost time, because of His goodness and mercy.

I'm so glad that God is not like man. He reigns over the unjust as He reigns over the just. God doesn't expect perfection from you before He blesses you. However, He will do some really special things for those who walk upright before Him. As matter of fact the Bible says, "…no good thing will he withhold from them that walk uprightly" (Psalm 84:11). We serve a God whose blessings will surpass your previous circumstances. It's the will of God that you and I prosper and establish success through Christ Jesus. True success lies within the presence of God. To be in God's presence "…is the (fullness) of joy; and (in God's) right hand there are pleasure for evermore" (Psalm 16:11).

If you really want to, you will do what's important to recover! Recovery and rebuilding your life requires having a strategy in place. Nehemiah rebuilt the wall of Jerusalem in fifty-two days (Nehemiah 6:15). His strategy: Nehemiah prayed and sought the Lord first (Nehemiah 1:1-11). Don't respond like the people who try to fix things by their own plans when they face trouble instead of going to the one who knows how to work things out. Nehemiah had to prioritize what was most important, he prayed and sought God's divine influence to lead and guide him.

Nehemiah was a king's cupbearer, which meant that he was the one who tasted the king's wine before the king drank it. If the wine was poisoned, then Nehemiah would die instead of the king. Since he already had a risky job, Nehemiah understood taking risks and what taking risks entailed. He took a risk and made a decision that he felt was important to him. Nehemiah left his post as cupbearer to do something about what had taken place in Jerusalem. He heard about how the gates were destroyed and how the city appeared devastated and unsafe. His spirit refused to believe that God would leave His people like that. Therefore, Nehemiah got up and did something about it. Nehemiah resigned as cupbearer to fulfill his divine purpose. It's time for you to rise up and to do something about your life, but don't forget to do what Nehemiah did first. Pray to God for direction.

Nehemiah is not really known for his accomplishments as a cupbearer, although his experiences as a cupbearer were important and could have been told. However, His life was more than his career as a cupbearer. He was passionate about his divine purpose and nothing was more important to him. Leaving his job as a cupbearer to follow what he believed to be his divine purpose would be considered an unpopular move to some people. I would suggest that if you are willing to make an unpopular move, then you should move with divine purpose in mind when you attempt to fulfill your destiny. Further, I'm not an advocate of leaving your place of employment on a whim. That was not what Nehemiah's story is about at all. This story is about doing what you know you're supposed to do in order to be a God-directed blessing to others. What you're supposed to do is what really counts in life. We are here for a purpose and that purpose is to fulfill God's will, not our own selfish desires.

Nehemiah understood that by making the decision he made, he would be talked about, laughed at and ridiculed. It didn't matter that his decision would be unpopular. Nehemiah was doing what he knew in his heart he was supposed to do. Nehemiah had to face his dilemma, because living in denial wouldn't fix it. You'd be surprised how many people actually live in denial. They refuse to accept the reality of the truth. Living in denial is like living blind when you have sight. When you live in denial, you walk into things unnecessarily and cause much harm to yourself. Often the hardest thing to do is to accept the truth for what it is. It's hard because the truth is not a nice thing to behold. You want to believe that your life will just work out without any effort on your part; that's living in denial. You see the problem, but you won't address the issue because of the confrontation that may take place; that's a denial. Admit that there is a problem then you can find a solution. "And ye shall know the truth, and the truth shall make you free" (John 8:32).

Nehemiah sought those who could assist him in his project because he knew he couldn't do it alone. God has assigned individuals to you to assist you in whatever He has given you to do. Never feel that you're in it by yourself. There are people that you would least expect who have the contacts and/or the tools you need. They may not have everything that you need, but they have something valuable for you. When you identify who these individuals are, you must allow them to share the necessary contacts and/or tools with you. People who are assigned to you don't have to be your close friends, but they are considered associates or people you work with. One of the problems that many people encounter is being close to people that they were never meant to be close to. The Bible tells us "...to know them which labor among you..." (1 Thessalonians 5:12). The purpose is to know where individuals belong in your life, so you can place them in the right place. This is an important lesson for you to learn. If you don't learn this, you'll try to assign people to the wrong places in your life. Some people are only to help support you for a season, not for your whole life. This can be a heart-breaking reality.

Repeatedly, I tried to make people fit within my scope, instead of allowing them to deliver only what they were destined to give for a specific season. I'm a person that loves people and loves holding on to good people. It's been very difficult for me to let people go, so God had to assist me in learning how to release people. I am a people's person, and I want people around me more often than not. This was extremely difficult for me when it came time for people to depart. It almost felt like someone died, because in my mind, it always appeared as loss and not a gain. I've grown spiritually, but in my office as an Apostle I had a problem sending and releasing people. The word Apostle means "sent one." Now isn't that ironic that I had a problem sending or releasing people and my office as an Apostle requires it? Well, many times that's the way it is. Whatever you're called to do, that's where you're the weakest. If you're called to minister to couples, you can expect your marriage to have some challenges. If you are called to minister to children, then you can expect challenges with your own children. They say preachers' kids are the worst kids. Well, that's not true all the time, but in some cases, it is. Sometimes it's even more than weakness in a particular area, because Satan attacks what you've been assigned to do. When you have been assigned to help people, sometimes people will fight against what you try to do. Some people would rather see you remain quiet and live unassumingly than for you to actively pursue change that will benefit an entire group. It's sad to say, but everybody doesn't want to see you rise up and pursue you destiny even if they might benefit from it in some way.

Once you have the people who are assigned to help you and you release those who are not, you have to recognize and avoid distractions. Nehemiah had to ignore all distractions in order to achieve what he was destined to do. Distractions will come, especially when you are passionate about doing something that will help others. It's easy to say, "It's not my responsibility to feed the poor" or "It's not my job to give clothes to the needy," but when you decide to extend yourself for the cause of others, you encounter many distractions some of which are personal distractions. Personal distractions are when you become distracted by your own stuff. Even your good stuff can distract you from your divine assignment. That's why it's so dangerous to build your satisfaction on your personal achievements and your personal belongings.

Your first purpose was to yield yourself to God, then, God equips and qualifies you to give to others. You and I live in a selfish-driven era in which everything is all about "me" and "mine." This is a crippling mentality. You must look out of your window so that you can see the needs of others. You must come out of your house so you can see that others don't have a house. Serving others may cause you some personal discomfort at times. You may serve others while leaving a trail of blood along the way. God may allow it to be that way, so others look down at your blood trail and say, "How can you do what you do for others while you need healing yourself?" Jesus bled while he was speaking and caring for his mother (John19:25-27). He bled while he told the malefactor on the cross, "Verily I say unto thee, To day (shall) thou be with me in paradise"

(Luke 23:43). Ministry is all about serving others while you yet have issues yourself. Don't let your issues in life distract you from helping others. If you focus on ministry and not on your personal problems, then you'll find that there are so many people that are worse off than you.

Opposition is inevitable, but retaliation is a must. If you don't retaliate, you will be defeated. Regardless of the type of opposition, it comes to try to force you to retreat and to cease from advancement. Nehemiah knew he had to fight while he was building. You have to have a Nehemiah attitude about what you want to do. You can't withdraw because you've been through too much already and you've come too far. Don't allow yourself to get to this point and then refuse to fight! Establish your words and your worship, so that you will not regress from expanding God's work and from living a full and complete life. Don't fight and not lay any bricks on the wall! Your life can't be focused exclusively on your enemies coming toward you. If you do, you'll wake up thinking about what people are saying about you and who doesn't like you. You'll be looking at what you don't have versus what others have. That time could be spent not only fighting against the enemies of your mind, but also rebuilding your life. It's about getting back what the devil stole from you and moving forward to achieve all that God has for you as well. It's about being rejuvenated, getting your drive back and believing that what looks impossible is probable.

If you can get this message nailed to your heart, then you have enough tools to work with to bounce back. In other words, it is while fighting that you can come to be like the Apostle Paul who said, "...for I have learned, in whatsoever state I am, therewith to be content" (Philippians 4:11). This can serve as the fuel for you as you navigate through life while trusting God along the way.

Nehemiah learned the necessity of consistency for completion. The story of Nehemiah is an awesome example of how a man, full of compassion, led by commission and driven by commitment displayed the qualities of leadership. Nehemiah should encourage you to overcome adversity so you can finish anything you set out to do in life according to God's will.

One thing I love about God is that He knows how to redeem the time. Remember, it only took Nehemiah, along with the people, fifty-two days to repair the walls of Jerusalem. That was approximately thirteen weeks to finish what appeared impossible to accomplish due to the opposition. God saved time and what normally would take much longer, didn't.

MY PERSONAL THOUGHTS ON CHAPTER 16

_____

_____

MY PERSONAL THOUGHTS ON CHAPTER 16 (CONTINUED)

_____

_____

_____

_____

_____

_____

_____

_____

_____

_____

_____

_____

_____

_____

_____

_____

_____

_____

_____

_____

_____

CHAPTER 17

GOD IS WAITING FOR YOU TO RECONNECT WITH HIM

2 Chronicles 7:14; Acts 17:30; 1 John 1:9; Revelations 2:5

The mind is the place where the conglomeration of thoughts filter through before settling and taking hold. The challenge is to prevent thoughts from settling and taking hold unless they are moving us ahead toward a closer walk with God or toward accomplishing what God has given us to do in life.

It appears that in each of our minds we have a set of principles that we live by. We live our lives either by what we've been told or by what we've learned on our own. These two methods can either move your life a step ahead for the better or hold you back. As believers, we are affected by our belief systems which were developed as a result of the principles we live by. Sometimes the principles we live by cause disconnection from God's plan for our lives. Disconnection is an enemy of destiny; it can keep you from moving forward.

We were not placed on earth to wonder around by ourselves. God did not design us to live life without people to influence our lives in some way or another. We are here to help each other live full and complete lives in Christ Jesus. I believe that God structured and placed the family unit on earth based upon the biblical principles He established in the Garden of Eden. According to the book of Genesis, God made Adam and Eve and they had children. I believe that's the set standard and example for families to follow: male (husband), female (wife), and children. When we move away from God's original plan for man, we develop disconnection. Two males can't produce children and two women can't produce children. We, as humans, were not made to marry someone that cannot or will not assist us in reproducing. This type of disconnection could cause the depletion of continued generations of children. If we disconnect from God's plan, we die. It's as simple as that.

No one gets around the principles that are necessary for progress. Principles are set and cannot be altered for convenience. If we expect progress, we must identify which principles will produce our desired results. We live in a society that wants everything quick and easy without any challenges or hard work. Progress takes the discipline that comes from challenges and hard work. We must make up our minds that whatever we have to do, we will do it.

One thing that we must do to progress is to establish standards for ourselves. No one can establish standards for us. Have you ever heard the expression, "You can lead a horse to water, but you can't make him drink"? We must become thirsty enough to do something different and to have something different. If we're not, then we'll sit by and watch others drink while we live the rest of our lives desiring more.

Dedication is another important aspect of progress. We must consistently stick with our goals until we accomplish them. This is where most of us have trouble. It's not the starting, but the follow-through where we sometimes have difficulty. Dedication is an absolute necessity if God is going to be glorified in our lives. It's through dedication that we grow and mature in life. It's through this principle that steps are taken to live a fulfilled life. Doing the same thing over and over again will give us the assurance that it can be done. We may get tired, frustrated and even bored doing things over and over again. When we repeat things over and over, we become better at them. As a result, we become more confident in doing the things that we do and we begin to think of new ways to do things better. This principle works in any field, on any job and on any task. It's the repetition of a thing that creates mastery. Michael Jordan's consistent practice and study of basketball caused his skills to develop to the level of greatness in the game. Michael Jackson's disciplined rehearsing caused his music, singing, and dancing to bring him to stardom. No matter what we do, if we want to be the best at it, we have to be dedicated to it. We must take our gifts and callings seriously as well. Whatever we are supposed to be doing, we need to do it to the best of our abilities. We cannot play with our gifts and callings. When we do, we take our destinies lightly. God gave gifts and callings to us for His glory and we are to use them to bless God and to bless others.

Progress takes determination. Determination is another quality that is necessary if we're going anywhere in life. It takes drive, dreams and diligence to take our destinies all the way. We must be self-motivated and have an unexplainable inner confidence that will push us forward. This is necessary because of the negativity that we face from day to day. We have to fight to stay focused every day. It's a fight to the finish, but we have to say, "I can do all things through Christ which strengthens me" (Philippians 4:13). I love it when I see someone dealing with crazy stuff like trying to raise a child as a single parent while going back to school and graduating with honors. That's awesome, because when someone accomplishes tasks like that, he or she is fueled to drive and go forward in life even more. There are too many weak people that just give up on themselves because of what happened to them in the past. They live in regret, based on what happened in their past. Nevertheless, my friend, it's not healthy for us to dwell in the past and not move on with our lives. Dwelling in the past will not get us anywhere. Why enter old age with frustration, anger, resentment, bitterness and hatred toward those who have moved ahead? I challenge you not to be among those who have died without birthing their dreams.

We must confront our giants even though it may be difficult. Difficult, but beneficial, and that's an understatement. Every destiny must confront giants. This is the inevitable. None can get around it. It's a part of the process. Before David faced Goliath, he had to defeat the lion and the bear first (1 Samuel 17:36). Nothing worth having comes easy. Even though God brought the children of Israel out of Egypt, they had to face enemies that were living in the wilderness. The wilderness was the route appointed by God that the Israelites had to travel through. Giants appear differently. They may not physically stand tall like Goliath, but they do stand tall in our minds, our marriages and in our finances. We cannot let the voices of our giants intimidate us. We cannot allow giants to present fear tactics that cause us to hold back and rethink our decisions. The size and the sound of our giants can't cause us to become stunned or stuck so that we won't move ahead.

Unhealthy attachments can cause us to miss great opportunities. It's like being single and having a close friend that's always there. Every time the single person is seen, he or she is always seen with his or her close friend. That close friend could be a distraction from finding a mate. People may either assume that the single person does not want to be bothered or that the single person is unavailable. That's possibly how it is when we're trying to figure out why we can't obtain greater opportunities in life. Perhaps it's because of unhealthy attachments that are connected to us. This is dangerous because no healthy person wants to be around sick people all the time. Sickness is not pleasurable and in some cases, it's extremely sad. Unhealthy attachments can drive blessings away from us. Therefore, we must be able to discern the difference between what is good and what is not good. It may have been good in a previous season, but not in this one. There is a time for every purpose and for every season, but when it's over, with tears running from our eyes, we must let go and acknowledge that it's over.

Don't get stuck and have an unbelievably challenging time letting go of people and things.

If you really want to progress utilizing the principles indicated in this chapter, you must come to God and He will in no way cast you out. "For the Lord will not cast off his people, neither will he forsake his inheritance" (Psalm 94:14). But, you must repent of your sins and acknowledge that Jesus is the son of God to be saved, accepted by God and to live with Him in eternity.

MY PERSONAL THOUGHTS ON CHAPTER 17

Chapter 18

God will get the glory out of this

Genesis 50:15-21; Job 42:12-17; Psalms 75:6-10;

Daniel 3:30

If God allowed us to do everything on our own, then He wouldn't get any glory out of anything. This may not make sense, but it's so true. God said that His ways are not our ways and He meant just that.

Job experienced being put in a difficult situation from which he could not extricate himself. It took God to get Job out of his dilemma. After Job's test, God gave him a new testimony and Job received a doubled blessing. The devil thought that if God removed the hedge of protection from around Job, that Job would curse God to His face. Even Job's wife said, "Dost thou still retain thine integrity? Curse God, and die" (Job 2:9). Even Job's wife felt that cursing God was the best way to get out of all the torment. Not Job! Job said, "Though he slay me, yet will I trust him" (Job 13:15) He also said, "If a man die, shall he live again? all the days of my appointed time will I wait, til my change come" (Job 14:14). That's exactly what Job did. As a result, God shocked everybody who knew Job. They were able to see his later situation and could attest that it was greater than his beginning.

God seeks to receive glory and honor out of all we go through in life. That's why He purposely designs circumstances to arise that only He can get us out of. I've experienced God's mighty hand of deliverance for myself.

My wife, my son and I almost drowned in the flood on Friday, June 23, 2010 in Hillside, Illinois. The water was rising while we were driving down Oakridge Avenue. It was between 1:00 am and 2:00 am. My son was driving my car and as he drove, we began to notice that the water was getting deeper and deeper. So I asked my son to backup, but he informed me that we should probably try and proceed forward, so we did. But, as we continued driving, the water began to rise and it got deeper and deeper. In a short time, it got so high that the engine shut off. After the engine would not start, I called 911 to inform them about the situation and I asked them to send a truck to pull us out. The truck company did not answer them; therefore, the woman on the phone told me to get out of the car. I kept insisting that she get a truck to pull us out and she kept on saying, "Sir, you need to get out of the car." Although she repeated this three times, I seemed to have been in a daze or in shock. I didn't move. I was trying to think through the process to see what I could do to save us. Then I began speaking in tongues, praying in the spirit while all this was going on. My son didn't want me to know that he couldn't get the engine to start no matter what he did. When I looked out the window, the water had risen all the way up to the top part of the door where the window began. It was almost up to my shoulder while I sat in my seat. My wife was saying that we needed to get out, but I was yet just trying to figure out what to do, without losing the car and without losing our lives at the same time. Then, I noticed that the water was beginning to seep into the car from the bottom of the door. I tried to open the door thinking that it was too late to wait for a tow truck to pull us out. Finally, I made up my mind to get out and walk through the water. However, when I went to tried to open the door, it was locked and there was no way humanly possible to escape. So there we were, sitting there trapped in the car and about to really panic, because none of the doors would open since the engine would not start. My son turned the key in the ignition again, and there was just enough power that traveled through to allow us to unlock the door and open it just in time. We got out of the car and by the time we came out of the water, I looked back to see the entire car go under as the water continued to rise. I believe God sent an Angel of Deliverance to release enough power to open the doors of that vehicle to save our lives. We felt helpless, but it took the supernatural power of God and His divine intervention to save our lives. If He had not sent His Angel, we would have lost our lives. It was the following week after our deliverance from the flood that God gave me the title and released me to write this book, *"Don't Tell Me It's Too Late."* This is what God did to get the glory out of my potentially devastating situation, just to bless others. Thanks be to God who has given us the victory through Jesus Christ, our Lord! He got the glory out of that whole situation.

God loves taking lives that appear hopeless only to lift them up so they can live again. He selects those who are the least expected; then cleans them, frees them and empowers them for His glory and honor. You may be one of those who is classified as the "least likely" to ever achieve anything of worth in life. But what an awesome position to be in! God can deliver you from any situation and make something beautiful and wonderful out of your life.

God uses the weak or those people who are rude, destructive, mean, evil and "flip-mouthed." He takes those individuals and gives them hope and direction. This is how God operates in order to show us how He makes models of mercy. He loves the rejected and those who are homeless and He gives them a new lease on life. He makes them prominent and successful as He did with Tyler Perry. Tyler Perry went from being homeless and a struggling playwright, to a multi-millionaire, playwright, actor and movie producer. What an encouraging example of how one can transition from poverty to prosperity!

MY PERSONAL THOUGHTS ON CHAPTER 18

_____

_____

_____

_____

_____

_____

_____

_____

_____

_____

_____

_____

_____

_____

_____

_____

_____

_____

_____

_____

_____

_____

_____

_____

CHAPTER 19

GOD'S PURPOSE WILL BE FULFILLED

Ecclesiastes 3:1; Jeremiah 1:5; Matthew 28:19-20; John 21:15-17; Acts 2:14-41

What a privilege it is to be chosen for God's purpose! It is awesome to know that God picked us to be part of a divine plan that's beyond our comprehensions. None of us should ever take that for granted. God didn't choose us once we were born into this world, but He chose us back before the world began to do something special for Him. That really is something to think about, and very comforting to know.

Think of all the things you've been through that were supposed to take you out of here, but couldn't; that alone is enough to make you shout! It means that God preserved you for His purpose, and for no other reason. Many don't acknowledge the responsibility that comes with the will to choose how they want to live. God didn't free the Israelites from the hand of Pharaoh to go into the Promised Land and live like they wanted to and to worship idol gods. He released them from bondage so that they could serve the true and living God. Some people think that no one can tell them what to do because they think, "I can live my life the way I want to live it!" However, it doesn't quite work like that.

Gifts and abilities have been placed inside of all of us so we will be a blessing to a specific individual or to a specific people for a specific time and a specific place. You are uniquely equipped with the grace, the ability and the tools to handle your specific God given role. You need to remember this because if you don't, you'll try to do things that others want you to do, but you're not graced to do. Being "graced" to complete a task means that you have the ease or the know-how to get the job done without making things worse. Grace is God making you able to do your assignment. Therefore, don't waste time allowing yourself to hold positions, to do projects or work in areas where you don't sense you are supposed to be for that season. I know that in order to bring a balance to this, we all must learn to wait for what God called us to do and to go through a preparation period, which is about submitting to leadership in our local churches.

Training is a necessity, as I believe that God has the local church and a Senior Pastor to help develop you into what He has called you to do. You must serve in your local church, and humbly serve in various capacities where you've been requested to serve by your Pastor. This is a very important lesson to learn, however, it may be humiliating at times. This training and service will be extremely beneficial for where God is taking you. If you can't serve another man's vision, you won't be in position for others to help assist you in achieving your vision or your purpose.

"He could have gotten someone else to do my assignment, but He chose me" is a statement that we often repeat in church. Well, you are right. He could have gotten someone else, but He didn't want anyone else; He wanted you. Aren't you glad to know that God sees value in you? People may not see your worth, but God does. Don't allow anyone to speak words to you that are not edifying. You must guard your heart by protecting your ears so you aren't listening to negative, pessimistic conversations that are not productive for the healthy state of your mind. You must protect your thought life, because it can determine how far you go in life. "Be renewed in the spirit of your mind" is what the Apostle Paul says to us in Ephesians 4:23. Each day you must be aware of all that comes to us whether by words, by sight or by sound. They all can have an effect on you. Depending on how you may feel at that time, all of these different things can clutter your mind and affect your emotions. So, it's of utmost importance to keep our minds renewed by the word of God.

I want to encourage you never to say that you're here by accident, because it was not an accident that you are here; you are born on purpose. Never again judge yourself based upon others' perceptions of you. They may not see you the way God sees you. But that does not negate the fact that you are who God says you are - that's what really matters.

It's time to be comfortable with the fact that you are the one He wants to use and it's not based upon you being perfect. You're not. We are all flawed and have shortcomings. If we had to be perfect, we would never be able to represent God or to do kingdom work.

You have what it takes to do the job. If you could really see yourself as God sees you, you'd be surprised. You've seen yourself based upon your failures, experiences and accomplishments. Most of us develop or base our belief systems upon this perspective. However, this is dangerous and detrimental for progress. It is dangerous to your destiny when failures, experiences and accomplishments determine who you are. Your good days and bad days should never speak to who you are and to what you're capable of achieving. Never allow ups and downs to become a fence to you, wherein you become trapped in your thinking. Do not let these things box you in and prevent you from being able to reach farther, higher and deeper into the wealth of your potential as a child of God. Satan wants to keep you looking at situations as though they are walls around you to hold you back. He wants to keep you believing that you can't go any higher, so he will make your problems appear like a roof that's been placed over your head.

No matter how difficult the job is that God has for you, you can do it. You can do it even if you have a horrible past that tells you, over and over again, that you are a failure. You can yet overcome all the odds that are against you. This is a new day with a new opportunity to start all over again. Feelings are sometimes destiny's worse enemy. Feelings have a way of painting a picture of deception in your thought process. If you allow your feelings to make decisions for you, then you are in serious trouble. Some people go through terrible things make decisions to do things that they're yet paying for and regretting. Never make important decisions based upon how you feel! Always wait, pray and seek God for guidance and counsel. Seek guidance from those who are Godly and knowledgeable in God's word to assist you in your decision-making process. You will be so glad that you waited before you made an additional mistake.

Never feel you are not qualified to represent God. You are qualified because you're His child. If He calls you, then you have already been justified or chosen to be the one. God doesn't make mistakes. We make mistakes. Just because you've made mistakes and it appears that your life has been a mistake or a joke doesn't mean that you are a mistake. We all have made mistakes but that doesn't mean that we, ourselves, are mistakes waiting to happen! People will make mistakes from time to time, but that doesn't cancel the purpose and plan that God has for you and I. The sad thing about it is that there are some people who know our mistakes and are there to remind us of them. But I want to encourage you to get up and move away from that type of environment, and to mix with people who will celebrate you and your destiny. Don't hang around toxic people that carry around your disease that you've already been cured of. Toxic people can influence you negatively because they are not healthy in their own characters. They like carrying diseases such as gossip. They love to slander the character of others, because it makes them feel good to know they have the scoop on someone and nobody has anything on them!

God has people, already in place, waiting on you to show up. I believe that they're called "destiny connections." They don't want to take anything away from you; all they want to do is help you get to your next dimension in God for the expansion of the kingdom. There are definitely kingdom-connectors, who don't mind sharing their resources with you and are not intimidated by your success. These are the people who are waiting to meet you. Open up your eyes so you can see that not everybody is against you. You don't want to live a paranoid existence, where you don't allow yourself to meet new people. But, be aware of their conversation and their characters to see immediately if they're toxic or kingdom-connectors. It won't take long. Pray and God will begin to show you by a sensing in your spirit whether it is a good relationship or not. If not, move on quickly, because you do not have any more time to waste. Destiny is calling for you to come, and to come now!

God's purpose in creation included you. Don't ever forget that in the beginning God created the heavens and the earth. Then on the 6th day He created man. He took the dust from the earth and blew into man's nostrils the breath of life and man became a living a soul. We are living souls because of the breath that was blown into Adam. We are the descendants of Adam. All that was in the nature of Adam is in our Adamic nature. However, when Adam sinned against God, he no longer had fellowship with God. Adam received a sinful nature. Therefore, Adam's descendants inherited that same nature even after Adam's fall. Jesus gave all those who believe that he is the Son of God his nature. Jesus is called "the second Adam." Therefore, if any man be in Christ Jesus, he is a new creature and old things are passed away. Behold all things are become new. (II Corinthians 5:17) We have, as believers in Christ Jesus, a brand new nature and a brand new beginning. The old nature is gone and the new is present within. This will take time to really understand and comprehend, but it's true. We have this treasure in earthen vessels that the Excellency of the power may be of God and not of us. Knowledge is power and truth is definitely an awesome treasure. Just the knowledge that God desires to use us with our limitations and human complexities is great within itself. There is a passage of scripture in the Bible that says, "My people are destroyed for a lack of knowledge." That means not knowing what God has placed within you can literally destroy your greatest potential. You can live and not ever come into utilizing your gifts and talents that He's given you. Knowledge opens up your mind to greater opportunities that are already present.

Knowledge leads you to the road where various people are located who will serve as tools or guides to lead you where you need to go in life. Close-minded people can only achieve what's in their minds already and what they presently see. The problem is that if they don't have anything new coming in, then after awhile, they become stale in their thinking. They become toxic, because now they feel self sufficient within. Such a person will only begin to become like a dinosaur. They believe that what they think is what everyone should think. If they are not careful, they will never move ahead to do great exploits for God. God said, "Behold, I will do a new thing; now it shall spring forth..." (Isaiah 43:19). This is how all of us should think and live. Each day when we get up, we should say, "This is the day which the Lord (has) made..." (Psalm 118:24). He made today for us to excel in it.

Likewise, we must not trap ourselves or hinder ourselves any longer. Believe that when He created the heavens and the earth, He did it with you and me in mind for a symbol of how much He loves each of us. He didn't want us to ever think that we are mistakes, or that we are placed here by accident. When He chooses us, He does such a marvelous thing. If God can throw stars in space, with billions of galaxies that can't be numbered, then He can handle our personal situations. If He can keep the solar system functioning and operating all in divine order, He can put our lives in order for His purpose.

Let there be a revolution that will cause you to rise up and break out of self-pity and passivity. It's now or never! Procrastination gets old. How long will you keep saying what happened to you earlier in life? People are tired of hearing it and you ought to be tired of saying it. I used to share with someone how I was recovering, but that person said, "I'm tired of you saying those words to me." That may sound harsh, but really that person was telling me that it's high time to move on with my life. That doesn't negate or disrespect the trauma or make light the fact that something was really painful, but how long will you sit there? There must be signs of irritation going on inside of you. If you're going to do great things for God, then you better begin preparing for it right now, like today!!!! You can't wait for anyone to validate you and affirm you. Stop waiting for a Prophet or fortune teller to tell you what you already know. It's up to you to make plans for a better life.

God wouldn't have had me write this book and for you to purchase it, if He wasn't speaking directly to you. He led you to buy it because it is ordained by God to help ignite the flame of the visionary and the dreamer within. I'm excited about your future and what you're about to do with the rest of your life. No more excuses, you have the rest of your life to birth everything that God placed within you.

MY PERSONAL THOUGHTS ON CHAPTER 19

_____

_____

_____

_____

_____

_____

_____

_____

_____

_____

_____

_____

_____

_____

_____

_____

_____

_____

_____

_____

_____

_____

_____

_____

IV. THE MIRACLE THRU OBEDIENCE

CHAPTER 20

GOD COMMANDS EZEKIEL TO PROPHESY TO WHAT'S LEFT

Ezekiel 37:1-10; Romans 4:17-21

You must take the necessary steps that God requires of you if you want to see the impossible become possible in your life. If you could have made something out of your life on your own, by now you would have already done it. If you could have worked every difficult thing out by now, you would have. There are many things that you are supposed to do for yourself, such as working or seeking knowledge by attending school to expand your learning. It's a whole different story when you get in a predicament and you don't know what to do and you don't know to where to turn. I've heard it stated for many years that God helps those who help themselves. There is some truth to that, but that statement is not the whole story. You are put here to do what you can, but when you can't do something then it's time to trust God for help.

God will allow you to be a part of unheard of circumstances and predicaments, and it may be difficult to explain how you got there. You may have arrived where you are because someone whom you trusted dropped you.

Someone could have let you down or left you without direction and contacts. It's most devastating to believe that people can be so cold. However, some people have experienced people behaving coldly toward them and some are experiencing it right now while they are reading this book. You may be faced with memories, faces and voices that torment you day and night. These memories, faces, and voices are there to remind you of what was and assist you in predicting what can't be in your future. You may be stuck with a bad memory and you want to believe that what's happened and where you are cannot be the end. You must live in a frame of mind that gives you fuel to go beyond where you are so you can see yourself differently. It takes faith to be able to keep you inspired and motivated while waiting until your change comes. You must believe beyond what you see and move forward until what you believe is achieved.

You must overcome the trauma of your present condition. This will be a fight, because you must confront all those negative desires and thoughts that you've allowed to settle within. It will take discipline to be able to destroy negative desires and thoughts and to dismiss them from residing within you. You must get sick and tired of accepting pain and making it a part of your life. Don't expect pain to remain. You can't keep pain from entering your life, but you can prevent it from being a permanent part of your life. You must quickly deal with your emotions and thoughts before they attach themselves to you as a lifetime partner. Some people actually live with pain as a crutch. It becomes a companion or a partner, because they're so used to having it there and getting sympathy and pity because of the pain. The only problem is that you remain dependent upon being miserable in order to get help. In many cases, there are people who really need others to depend on because they have physical disabilities. I'm not referring to those situations. I am talking about people are crippled in their thinking and are comfortable being that way because they can get "hand-outs." This only hurts you and no one else.

First of all, you must see that you need help. In Luke 15:11-32, the prodigal son had to first come to the end of himself. He was about to eat as the pigs ate. It got so bad until he said, "I don't have to live like this my father has hired servants." Then, he got up from where he was and went home to his father's house. His restoration did not begin until he came to himself and got up willingly to go to get help. This is what I'm saying to each of you: Help is there, but you must first rise up and stop crying over where you are. You may be living in the midst of family members who just don't care about a positive future. They're okay with selling drugs and/or prostituting their bodies. Some may be alright with gambling all their monies away and taking unwise risks for gain. It's really up to you if you want to continue carrying on a generational curse, which is the same spirit, attitude and sin that's been done throughout your family for generation after generation. You don't have to live with an abusive mentality. There's help for you. You can overcome what appears to be chained to you. You may live where there's fighting, cursing, cheating on companions, adultery, fornication or all sorts of perversion. You don't have to be a product of your environment. You can live life to the fullest, knowing that Jesus has your cure and you can have a victorious life.

Ezekiel was a prophet in Ezekiel 37:1-14 who was sent by God to inform a nation of people that their future was going to be brighter than what they saw. So, Ezekiel had a vision of a valley full of dry bones, and the valley was very full. Ezekiel understood the perplexity of being in a position of seeing only devastating things right before his very eyes. Whether it's right before your eyes or right in your face, it's different than just hearing about it, or seeing others go through something that's crazy. It's a whole other thing when you have to face devastation or deal with it yourself.

You must get up every day with great expectation for what's next. You must believe that deep within there is a reason why you're dealing with this! I've learned that nothing we experience is a waste, not even our mistakes. All things work together for good, to those who love God and to those who are the called according to His purpose (Romans 8:28). That's the key. God's purpose for your life is that He allows things to happen. Learn how to encourage yourself in the Lord. If nobody says positive things concerning you, then stand in the mirror each day and speak the word of the Lord over your own life. God said in Jeremiah 29:11, "I know the plans that I have towards you, plans of peace and not of evil, to prosper you and not harm you, and plans to give you a future full of hope." You can have a future full of hope and not a future full of regret, even though it presently looks hopeless. Make up in your mind that it's not going to end like this, even though like Ezekiel you see bones and you don't see life anywhere. As a matter of fact, like Ezekiel, you're kicking bones and shoving bones around. We've all visited the cemetery many times, but none of us want to remain there. The cemetery is for those who are dead, not for the living. When you go to bury someone you love, you never plan to live there. You're just there to deposit the dead into the ground. Well, it's time to deposit those dead things into the ground so you can leave them there and go on to live.

Be ready and willing to do what you must do now. Some people are too stubborn and set in their ways to consider something different than what's been and what is. This might be the death of the people who continue to rebel and do not allow themselves to be challenged to think differently. It is different thinking that could bring you to the reality of great possibilities and potential. Let this mind be in you which is also in Christ Jesus. Believers are warned not to get stuck in thinking how they thought in the past. It's easy to recoil, which means to move back and to retreat.

This is also not the time to stand thinking about what to do when you already know what to do. Just step out by faith and have the willingness to make moves. The word is the willingness to do it. You must be willing and obedient to do what's required of you in order to excel in life. God has set standards, which are put in His word for each of us to live by. If we follow them, we get positive results. If we don't, we get negative results. It's plain and simple. If you turn right, then you'll go to the right. If you go in the wrong direction, then you'll get turmoil and setbacks. You wouldn't believe how many people hold themselves back just because they refuse to do what's required for progress. My heart goes out to those people who've been lied to and believe that it's over because of the present or the past circumstances. That's what Satan does.

Satan steals, kills and destroys your confidence in believing that it's actually possible to do what God says you can do. If you buy into it, then Satan's got you and you'll be held as a prisoner of doom. As a believer, you are a prisoner of hope. You have this hope in God's ability through Christ Jesus that you can do all things, because He strengthens you. He always causes you to triumph. This should give you strength and hope to wake up every day believing that something great is about to happen. Hope gives you great anticipation to strive to always be willing and ready to learn and to meet others who can pour into you during your process of development. I believe a willing mind is the start for the beginning of a new life. If there's no will power, then a way will not open for you. That thought is enough for an entire book by itself! You can literally educate yourself and gain degrees in how to build architectural structures. There is also technological training for those who want to become engineers and want to develop machines. However, if you have all of the knowledge but you don't begin to implement it, then you went to school for naught.

Knowledge has power when it's implemented like faith without works is dead. Some people have the will to learn the lesson, but don't have the will to make the lesson become practical. You must do it, even if it doesn't make sense. Ezekiel, the Prophet, was standing there, looking at what seemed like the end. God said to him, "Can these dry bones live?" This was quite an unusual way for God to begin the dialogue. Even though it was a vision, God knew that only He could do what Ezekiel or any other man couldn't do, but yet He asked Ezekiel the question. Anytime God asks questions, He's not asking as though He doesn't know the answer and needs a human being, who He made, to give Him an answer! Absolutely not; He asked the question to see how Ezekiel saw the situation. This is powerful in itself, because it isn't like God to allow us to go through things to see if we'd respond properly or if we learned previous lessons of the past. He wanted to see, first of all, how Ezekiel saw it. Maybe some of the problem is not seeing things correctly - not seeing it as an opportunity for God's phenomenal ability to be demonstrated. God always wants us to always see Him as able. He doesn't ever want us to see Him as crippled or incapable of handling difficult situations. God also wanted to hear what Ezekiel had to say. Based upon his words, God gave Ezekiel permission to keep speaking to Him and giving Him the directions that he needed to bring resolution to his dilemma.

Your perception and your words have a lot to do with whether or not you are willing. Most of the time, you can figure out a person pretty quickly once you get them to talk. It's those of few words that are sometimes difficult to understand.

Ezekiel responded to God, "Lord thou knows." This was the right thing for him to say. He passed the test, because he didn't think that he had the answer. If he had tried figure it out with a human perspective, God would know that he wasn't viewing his circumstance correctly. But he said, "Lord, you know!" That's the answer that all of us should have when our backs are up against the wall – "Lord, you know." He's the only one who can get you out of the problems you're having. It will not make sense to you, but God doesn't have to make sense with anything He does. The fact that He chose you and I doesn't make sense, because we know ourselves and our weaknesses. It doesn't make sense that He loves us so much, just because. I'm yet trying to figure that out: He loves us and He continues to love us. However, the fact that He willingly chose you should make you willing to do whatever He says to do. You must apply faith and let God do the rest. It will definitely take God to accomplish the things that need to be done. Therefore, faith must be applied in order to get it done.

When you consider the success of others, you're probably shaking your head and saying to yourself, "How in the world can God use me, and how can I overcome the shame that everybody knows about?" It's going to take one hundred percent, total reliance and trust in God. That's the only option. If there's baggage in your life that's weighing you down, then you have to get to the place where you say, "I don't care anymore" and "By faith, unload!" That's where you have to be before you are ready to walk by faith and not by sight. You must unload, detach and defuse everything that's plaguing you, before you blow up. The inner conflict of the soul can bring such disturbance to life that, if not careful, you'll stay stuck in unbelief because of the season that you're in right now.

Ezekiel had to trust that if God had brought him to this point in his life to see all of the chaos before him and bones all around, then something would come out of it. Can you imagine what it was like to be in that predicament, not knowing the full existent of the purpose of the situation?

But when Ezekiel said, "Lord, you know," God knew he was ready for his next assignment. God is trying to bring you to a place of readiness for your assignment. He doesn't want you to live in shock over where you are right now in life. He doesn't want you to be mesmerized by your divorce or loss any longer. Yes, there will be a period of time where grief is normal. It's the same with the loss of loved ones you've lost that you loved so dearly. Life brings tragedy and we are tossed back and forth by what life brings each day. However, there must be a time after those deeply sad experiences where it's time to rise, even if your grieving period may take a little longer than others. I never want to appear to be insensitive to the pain, the agony and the disappointments that have taken place in anyone's life. But I am saying, "Don't allow your wounds to remain open to the point that you are not useable for God's glory." Do what you must do. But, whatever you do, please don't give up on God and don't give up on life. If you are struggling over situations, I want to encourage you to take small steps by faith. But, please move! People who don't move show signs of death. Everything that lives must move! It was God's design for things to move! If you don't move by God's word, then you take the risk of ending up like those who died in the valley that Ezekiel saw. If you have the spirit of faith as Ezekiel did, then God will do the rest.

Don't be surprised at what may take place when you walk by faith and in accordance with God's plans for your life. It may be a type of shaking, and a whole lot of noise before it begins to make any kind of sense. Along with the noise will be necessary movement, meaning that there will be people and things that will move away from you and which could potentially cause you pain. At the same time, God could have you moving and changing so you can begin connecting to people who are sent by Him to help you get to your purpose. We are living in perilous, but exciting times. We are in the midst of killings. Standards are being lowered in the church and everywhere in society. Yet, God is able to resurrect your dreams, visions and bless you abundantly, even during a recession. He can raise the dead. He has done it in the Bible days, as well as in these days. I'm speaking of those who have lost their inspiration and aspirations. God gave me the desire to write this book so that you can gain, believe again, and hope again. There's yet some worth left, even in you. Don't be surprised where it is that God is taking you. One day God spoke these words to me, "*I'm going to show you what 'out' looks like.*" You can be in so much turmoil and confusion that you don't see any way out. God told me that He was going to show me what "out" looks like. Some of you have forgotten what "out" looks like, but He's about to show you the other side of "in" and it's called, *"OUT!"* A brother told me that God told him to tell me, "*The rest of your days will be the best of your days, both naturally and spiritually.*"

The church where I am Pastor went through many devastating losses. Some were of God and some were not. Some members left because it was God who was leading them and others left just because they wanted to leave. However, when they left, it almost crippled the entire ministry, which was beginning to dwindle down at an alarming rate. I begin to wonder what was happening. We were striving to please God and to do what He said to do. We had pipes bursting and water flooding into the auditorium. You could have glided across the front of the church on a surfboard. I felt like the Apostle Paul with trouble on every side! That's just the way it was. It seemed I kept getting calls about something going wrong with the building. We had purchased a theatre, and of course, as with any building, there were complications. Repairs were needed. People were leaving the church and the finances were dropping, although the bills were remaining the same. Somehow and some way, God sustained us through it all.

I didn't know which way to go, and before I knew it I begin to slip into a place which I call "border line bitter." I was not handling my feelings the way I should have about my situation. I do understand that life can hit you like that, but staying that way doesn't change anything. Time went by and I didn't want to fellowship or to hang around with the saints like I used to. I went into a shell. Before I knew it, I was stuck. While I was preaching I was fighting voices that were saying, "It's over, look at the crowd. It's over, look at the offering. It's over." I continued to Praise God by faith, even when my feelings tried to dictate otherwise. I didn't know when the next tragedy was going to take place. I was in a very unimaginable season, yet I had to walk and speak and smile on the way out the door each Sunday. Still, on the inside, I was aching. I said, "Lord, how long? What should I do to get help to maintain?"

I was compelled by God to get up early in the morning to pray around 4 a.m. or 5 a.m. for clear directions. On one day, I remember standing at my front window in my office very early in the morning. For a few weeks I was led to begin reading, over and over again, the 37th Chapter of Ezekiel about the valley of the dry bones. I heard the voice of God talking to me one day while I was staring out of my window. He said these words: "Prophesy to what's left!" That sparked something on the inside of me and gave me hope to take what was left and get back to strengthening the house.

I want to pause here for those Pastors who may be in the same state that I was in. You may feel that people have mistreated you; preachers have mistreated you; the members, trustees and deacons have mistreated you; and you feel like giving up. Wait! Before you stand in the pulpit to resign because you're saying, "I just can't take it anymore!" I want you to take authority over the powers of darkness and begin to prophesy to what's left. Even if it's a few, speak into their lives and develop them. Select a few who have your heart and train them. Don't give up on your assignment, because God called you to it! Believe that there are people who are assigned to you and you can't give up like that. Please allow God to speak into your life and let Him renew your hope. Find someone that genuinely supports you and gather prayer partners who will pray you through during this season, because you need to believe again in your ministry. You need to believe that you yet have what it takes to start all over again. Find someone who can make your baby leap! Not a natural baby, but the dream that you envisioned years back! You need that baby to leap again, just so you can see and believe that your baby is not dead! God gave it to you. You just got side-tracked because of everything that happened. Because I've been speaking to every area that needed the bones to connect, they've been connecting and strength has been coming to the overall ministry of our church.

I remember reading in the Bible in Jeremiah 33:7,11, where it says, "It will be as it was at first!" When I saw that at least twice, I began to see what God was saying to me. It would be as it was at first. I believe that it will be was it was at first and even greater, but I needed to hear that it will come back again. This is what someone who is reading this book needs to know. It is God who is saying directly to you that it will come back again. Stand in faith, no matter where you are and where you've been. He will put your life back on course again. It may have been side-tracked, but He will redeem the time in order to get you back on course.

Start Praising God, and believe that what was dead shall come back because God said it would! Your hope, your drive, your inspiration, your vision and your dreams are all a part of your destiny. The act of Praising God shows Him that you acknowledge His ability to do great and impossible things. Praise makes you see how awesome He's been in the past, and makes you view Him as capable of doing this for you as well. Never complain, but always speak well of God before God and before men. In everything, we are to give thanks! We must train ourselves to do give thanks, because it's right to do and it pleases God when we do it. While you're praising God, it will help take your focus off of how bad things appear. It has a way of softening the blows that come against you from day to day. Psalms 150 says, "Let everything that hath breath, Praise the Lord, Praise ye, the Lord." So while you're Praising God, it will give you a new lease on life to believe again, even though nothing has changed. Those who are believers in Christ Jesus must not only praise God, but believe that through the power of Jesus Christ all things are possible to them that believe. It's very hard to do it when you don't feel up to it, but just do it anyway. Praise your creator and believe He will make a way for you while you're praising Him.

If you pray in faith, you'll begin to sense slight movements of restoration. It might not be what you were looking for all at once, but there will be movements. Your vision may appear to be slow in coming, but despise not the days of small beginnings. You must learn how to praise God when there are only tiny signs of change for the good. That simply means that God is answering your prayers and change is slowly beginning to take place. Those are the signs of recovery. Magnify what is taking place and don't complain about what's not taking place. If you continue to trust God, there will be total restoration in your life and in your ministry. But you've got to hold on and kept the faith no matter what. Keep doing what you need to do and expect every area in your life to come back to order, because God said it would. That's what you stand on.

God said to Ezekiel, "Prophesy to the bones, and they shall live." That was good enough for the Prophet to stand on, because if God said it, Ezekiel knew that it was possible. The nation of Israel had been taken captive by enemies, who took them away from their home land and held them captive for seventy long years. But through this vision, God was giving hope to His people by showing Ezekiel that it won't stay like that. God's got a plan! This is what your attitude must be like. "God's got a plan for my life" is what you've got to hold on to. Every word He's saying to you is in His word and He will back up what He says at all times! Get ready for your new beginning, because God always backs up what He says. I am a witness that you can recover. It may look like a cloud the size of a man's hand, but it is going to rain, because God said it.

You may have to keep looking up like Elijah and his servant did, but if you keep looking, the cloud is going to swell and fill the sky until it is so heavy with rain that it falls upon the scorched and dry ground where all vegetation had been demolished. It was over three and a half years with no rain. Starvation was everywhere. It looked hopeless once again, but when it was time, it rained. Well, people of God, it seems like it's about that time again for rain to fall upon us. He said He would restore to you the years that the locus hath eaten. God allowed a period of time for famine to take place throughout the Old Testament. It kept appearing, but every time God provided for His people. If He says, "It's a new day and I'm going to allow my blessings to rain upon your life naturally and spiritually," then expect it. Don't doubt it, for it will surely come to pass.

The Prophet's heart must have been leaping as he heard noise and looked up to see movement taking place. It may have appeared as a mass display of confusion while it was taking place. But it didn't happen until the Prophet opened his mouth and obeyed God. When he did, something began to take place.

MY PERSONAL THOUGHTS ON CHAPTER 20

_____

_____

_____

_____

_____

_____

_____

_____

_____

_____

_____

_____

_____

_____

_____

_____

_____

_____

_____

_____

_____

_____

_____

Chapter 21

God Moves when you move and God speaks when you speak

Proverbs 18:21; Mark 11:23-24; Matthew 18:18

If you do nothing, nothing will happen. If you allow yourself to start something, you will feel that you're under pressure to make something happen. Nothing moves until you speak. Nothing is accomplished in your life until you do something yourself. God is not going to do everything for you.

I came to the reality that God is not going to do everything for you when I was standing at my front window, pondering what I should do. I had to decide that I would make the first move. When I did make the move, I was surprised at what I found. I found that what was left in the house was what I needed for that season. I had qualified individuals right under my nose. Even though I didn't know it, it didn't mean that God didn't know it! He sees and knows all things, and I had to come to a place of frustration so God could speak to me and give me further direction. As I prophesied to what was left, I found out that what was left was sufficient for me and the ministry. I'm so grateful to God for giving me what I needed for that season. I had to adjust to the new ministry gifts, their methods and their styles of ministry. This taught me that when new ministry gifts or new people come into your life, you have to adjust just as they have to adjust.

Some leaders have a hard time letting go of the people they had and try to function as though the individuals are still present. Other leaders keep the people they have and don't allow new people, fresh ideas and new innovative concepts to enter their lives, because new ideas will challenge you to change for the better. You can't be fearful about change or embracing the new. Whether we like it or not, change is inevitable. I remember growing up in Maywood, Illinois in the 60's. The streets were laid with brick blocks, but time brought about a change and now the streets have black top. Everything changes, with you or without you. God will not allow us to stand in the way of change just because things have been a certain way in the church or in our lives. It's a requirement to behold new things, so you should keep expecting better and wanting new things to enter into your life. Now, it's your turn. God is waiting for you to make the next move. The longer you procrastinate, the longer you have to wait for God's best blessings to come to you. He operates by principles like: Give and it shall be given unto you (Luke 6:38) and If ye be willing and obedient, ye shall eat the good of the land (Isaiah 1:19). It's your move, because God has given each of us a measure of faith to get things accomplished.

When I began moving, I developed or restructured all the areas of the church. Now, I have a tremendous working operation in my ministry. I've been the Pastor of the Progressive Life-Giving Word Cathedral for twenty-seven years. We currently reside in Hillside Illinois. I had to learn how important it was for me to make the next move as it refers to progress. Isn't it ironic that God would have my father, Dr. James B. Alford, Sr., come to the little village of Maywood, Illinois in the mid-forties to look at a building that was leaning sideways? He had to have the building reconstructed and had to put a basement underneath it. Nevertheless, while it was leaning, God spoke to him and said, "Name the church, 'Progressive Church of God in Christ'" and he did. At the time my Father became Pastor, the church's name was, "The Church of God in Christ of Maywood." God showed my father that the ministry was all about progress. Even though the building was leaning, it didn't mean that what was leaning couldn't straighten up and stand erect to progress. Prophetically, the church was destined to progress, so he changed the name. In the year 2010, the church celebrated its 85th Anniversary and we are still progressing, and living up to that most powerful predestined name.

A quick response in obedience causes a quick reply. There are so many times when we stop and think too much about what we already know we're supposed to do. This is detrimental to your future, and will only hinder you, because, it allows the devil to have room to talk to you and give you reasons why you should wait. Waiting is important and necessary only when God says to wait, but if God says to go, waiting is out of the question. Do what God says when He tells you to! A delayed response is a sinful response and you must repent for it, because He told you to do something within a specific time frame. If He called you to preach the word of God, then answer the call and submit under your Pastor for preparation for that call. However, you can't start running revivals and camp meetings around the country without being prepared and equipped. You must allow time to walk in certain offices and ministry gifts. This is not waiting outside of God's timing; this is spending time preparing for what God desires you to do. I was speaking of those things that you can do immediately. You're not to wait when you know it is God telling you what to do.

When you oversleep and you are running late for work, you probably wanted someone to knock on your door a little harder to wake you up. Some people sleep so deeply that they can't sense any noises at all. That's when somebody needs to knock harder, because the person who is sleeping deeply can't sense that it's late. Knocking hard feels like my assignment to you. I pray that you hear the hard knock or that an alarm is ringing in your spirit, letting you know it's high time to wake out of your sleep. I command you to be shaken on the inside and rise up with vigor and vitality so you can respond quickly in obedience to do all God has called you to do. Only you can make this decision.

MY PERSONAL THOUGHTS ON CHAPTER 21

_____

_____

_____

_____

_____

_____

_____

_____

_____

_____

_____

_____

_____

_____

_____

_____

_____

_____

_____

_____

_____

_____

_____

_____

_____

CHAPTER 22

GOD WANTS YOU TO EXPECT SIGNS OF RECOVERY

Mark 15:17; Luke 17:11-19; John 5:1-9

Proper positioning and connections fitly join together the body of Christ (Ephesians 4:16). It's important as you speak and move forward in faith that you don't hook up with the wrong people. Don't allow your excitement about things finally moving to deceive you or to catch you off guard. You want to make sure that whomever you connect with is a destiny connection that will assist you with the necessary tools for your destiny. Also, you want to make sure that the destiny connections are the individuals that you are to assist as well. This is crucial and must be viewed as one of the most important principles to have.

The spirit of deception doesn't appear deceiving with the natural eye. Sometimes, people who are raving wolves come in sheep's clothing. Try their spirits by the spirit of God within you and by the word of God based upon their conversations and beliefs (1John 4:1). Assessing the characters of potential destiny connections is important as well. It may take time to really see who people are, so don't bring a person you don't know into your personal life too quickly. Only discuss business and keep it short and to the point. As the Holy Spirit leads, that's how you should follow. He will lead you and guide you into all truth (John

16:13). Always remember, he will not lead you into error or deception. Don't get caught up with individuals who are highly gifted, talented and self-absorbed. You can't afford to connect with the wrong people in this hour. You've been waiting too long to be tricked by the enemy. So, take your time. Pray and fast, if necessary, to make sure that they're the right connections. They may have some of what you need, so embrace them, learn from them and give to them, so they can glean from you. We are helpers to one another. Yet, everyone we help may not be a destiny connection.

Ezekiel watched how the bones connected in his vision. The right bones connected with the right joints until the entire skeleton had its bones in the correct positions for the next miracle to happen. The next miracle was the sinews on the bones, then flesh appeared and finally, the skin appeared (Ezekiel 37:1-10).

Proper positioning may take a little time, because the one you need to connect with may be in another city or state. Also he or she could be right in your face, but he or she is not ready to connect with you. God has to get him or her prepared to connect with you. So don't be frustrated that while everything else seems to be coming together, the thing that you really want to happen isn't. In time, it will.

When people who are not right try to be a part of your life, it's like a three-way plug trying to connect into a two-way outlet. It just won't fit, because it wasn't designed to fit.

That's how many of us are - people who are three-way plugs, trying to fit into the two-way outlets. We keep trying to connect, but we just can't. So learn to let go of trying to make things work that are not supposed to work out.

When you begin doing things God's way, there will be signs that show a change in your attitude and in your spirit. It's like the dead Israelites whose bones Ezekiel saw. They began to stand on their feet as a mighty army and so will you. Know that the way you've been will no longer be, because you're about to stand tall and be a force to reckoned with. People will have to readjust their thinking about you, because a new you will begin to blossom and unfold like a flower. People are used to you being bent over from carrying so many woes in your life. Congratulations! You are about to rise up and get a new posture where your countenance, your expression and your attitude will begin to change right before people's eyes. You will have to get used to this new you and it will take some time. But be alright walking around smiling when no one is telling jokes. Be all right singing around the house when no music is playing. Be okay lifting your hands, shouting and praising God while taking a walk.

This is the beginning of a new season, and a new day. Just walk into your season of joy and bliss. This will be a wonderful expression of God's love and peace that He's bestowed upon you. As you continue to walk in obedience to God's word, you'll see more and more signs of restoration in your life.

There may be some who say that there's nothing changing in you or about you. However, your change isn't based upon your getting them to see it, as long as you can see it. That's all that matters. God is about to help you, revive you and cause you to rise up like never before so you can do more than you've ever thought you could do, because of your obedience. God said, "If (you are) willing and obedient, ye (will) eat the good of the land" (Isaiah 1:19). You are about to get up from there and stand tall, because you're about to eat!

MY PERSONAL THOUGHTS ON CHAPTER 22

_____

_____

_____

_____

_____

_____

_____

_____

_____

_____

_____

_____

Chapter 23

Whatever you do, don't quit now...it's not too late!

Psalms 118:17; Psalms 118:24; 1 Kings 7:3; John 9:4; Luke 19:13; Romans 13:11-14

I'm praising God because On Friday, October 1, 2010 at approximately 1:40 p.m., at the Doubletree Hotel, while running a two-day Fall Revival for Center for Hope Church, in Bloomington, Illinois, where the Senior Pastor, Bishop Larry Taylor & First Lady Desetra Taylor serve –

I Finished This Book!

You must stop listening to negativity - it can destroy your creativity. It is also very detrimental to your progress. Run away from those who bring mental clutter. They bring it and place it on you to deal with while they walk away from it.

When Nehemiah, cupbearer for the king, was repairing the damaged walls of Jerusalem, someone came to him saying that he needed to come down to deal with the gossip of people and what they were saying about him. His response was, "Oh no. I'm not coming down to deal with that. I'm doing a good work and I can't come down." That's the same type of response you must have when your enemies want to tell you what people are saying about your life or your ministry. You have to stand bold in this hour; look them in the face and say, "Absolutely not, I am doing a good work, God is about to do great things in my life. Oh, no; I'm not coming down for people who were never for me. I'm not coming down to tell about my shortcomings."

Oh, no, you don't need anyone from your past to disturb the mind you have to succeed and defeat the enemy. There are those who have been sent by Satan himself to slow down your zeal and drive. They are there to make you think about what people are saying so you think twice about your assignment. You're too close to something special that will help others move ahead in life. What God is about to do for you is mind-boggling! Your eyes have not seen, nor have your ears heard and neither has it entered into the heart of man the good things that God has prepared for them that love God and who are the called according to His purpose for their lives. What a mighty God who gives strength and power to enable you to accomplish great things for His glory!

Whatever you do, fight to ignore all voices and sounds of scornful laughter sent by the devil and others. Let them talk and hold conversations by themselves, because there's too much at stake. You have come too far. You are at the crossroads of destiny. This is your turning point, so you can't turn back now. Why read this book and get to the last chapter, then say, "Oh well, I still think it's too late?" You can't quit. There are too many others depending on you to survive. You were not created to quit; you were created to win! You have what it takes to defeat all of the enemies that stand in the way of your destiny.

Greater is He that is in you than He that is in the world. In Christ, Paul wrote in Romans 8:37, "that we are more than conquers through him that loved us." If God be for us, who can be against us? You must have the attitude that, "In thee Oh Lord do I put my trust!" These are the sayings that should come out of your mouth. Refuse to think defeat or to speak defeat. Rise up and say, "Enough is enough. If it's a new day, then it's another chance to do awesome things for the kingdom with God's help." Stop regretting opportunities that are no longer available and feeling that nothing else positive will come to pass for you. This is a definite concern that I have for so many people. They feel that based upon what they had and what they lost, there's nothing new that can come into their lives.

I can really understand why Paul said, "Forgetting those things which are behind and reaching forth to those things which are before, I press toward the mark of the prize of the high calling of God, which is in Christ Jesus. Forgetting is not humanly possible in some cases, once you've experienced things personally. However, I believe that the Apostle is saying that God wants you not to ponder over past experiences to the point that they become tormenting thoughts. Tormenting thoughts can develop into strongholds that live with you just to irritate you. The way you strive to forget is by replacing bad thoughts with new, better thoughts. Let this mind be in you which is also in Christ Jesus. Meditate on the word, day and night, and you shall be like a tree planted by the rivers of water that will bring forth fruit in his season, and his leave shall not wither and whatsoever he doeth shall prosper. You must have healthy thoughts. The word of God brings the transformation you need to overcome as you change how you think from day to day. Get up each day and speak out of your mouth, "This is going to be a tremendous day for me and for my family." Remember, death and life are in the power of the tongue.

Imagine stretching yourself higher, farther and doing more than you've ever done before. Expect greater opportunities to come your way. Live your life with an attitude of faith knowing that, because you are God's child, He has so much more to give you. Never allow anybody or anything to paint the picture in your mind that your day or your time is over. You must "Fight to think right." I said, "Fight to think right," because this is exactly what you have to do! If you're going to do great things, then you will have to think great thoughts that will cause great things to come to you. Whatever you do, please protect your mind. Don't allow what you see and what you hear to paint a picture of gloom and doom for your life. No matter what comes your way, you must yet say that the devil meant it for evil, but good is coming out of it. Keep speaking positive things although tears are running down your face and/or you're walking the floor because you can't sleep at night. Say it until you see it come to pass. It will surely come to pass. Though it tarry, wait for it. Paint your own picture with the word of God. Take one chisel as a sculptor would, and strike your situation with scriptures until you clearly begin to see what God said more than what the devil is trying to say. Don't curse yourself and speak the benediction over your life or your destiny. What your enemies are waiting for you to do is to curse yourself. To speak damnation or to speak and proclaim your own destruction would be a travesty and it is not an option. It cannot happen.

I believe that now you've crossed over to the other side where you're beginning like never before to see yourself in a different light. Rise up and shout loud to everything that serves as an enemy of your new day. Say this: "Don't Tell Me It's Too Late!" I want you to become violent in your actions towards the enemies of your soul and begin by saying, singing and shouting and even dancing, if you must, that it's not over. Tell the devil. Be bold and say, "Don't tell me it's too late, because it's not too late. I serve a God that will give another chance, not just a second chance, but chance after chance after chance."

When I began prophesying to my own situation and began speaking in faith, God began giving me a recovery plan. He began showing me, step by step, what to do. He could not do this until I was ready to move on. Aren't you ready to move on? Aren't you sick and tired of being sick and tired? Is crying or getting an attitude with God and others changing your situation? You need God to give a recovery plan. Have the courage to see yourself thriving, excelling, achieving and growing in every area of your life and in your ministry. Whatever you do, don't die like this. No matter what mistakes you've made in life and no matter how old you are, rise up, man or woman, and tell the devil, "It's not too late - a new life can begin!"

After finishing the rough draft for this book, I got up the next day, and had my devotional time. The Lord took to me to the book of Zephaniah 3:17-20 and began to speak to me out of His word and this is what He said, "The Lord, thy God, in the midst of thee, is mighty. He will save and He will rejoice over thee with joy. He will rest in His love. I will joy over thee with singing. I will gather them that are sorrowful for the solemn assembly, who are of thee, to whom the reproach of it was a burden. Behold, at that time I will undo all that afflict thee: and I will save her that halted, and gather her that was driven out; and I will get them praise and fame in every land where they have been put to shame. At that time will I bring you gain even in the time that I gather you: for I will make you a name and a praise among all people of the earth, when I turn back your captivity before your eyes, saith the Lord." I believe He is telling us to rise up and tell the devil, "Don't tell me it's too late," because if God says that we can have a new beginning, then that's all that matters.

MY PERSONAL THOUGHTS ON CHAPTER 23

_____

_____

_____

_____

_____

_____

_____

_____

_____

_____

_____

_____

_____

_____

_____

_____

_____

_____

_____

_____

_____

_____

_____

_____

_____

_____

DESTINY GUIDE   JANUARY
GOD'S CHANNEL OF PREPARATION IS TRANSITION.

Write down a list that categorizes the areas in your life that are difficult to deal with and where transition is needed for the better (for improvement):

_____

_____

_____

_____

_____

_____

_____

_____

_____

_____

_____

_____

_____

_____

_____

_____

_____

_____

DESTINY GUIDE   FEBRUARY

GOD'S ASSIGNMENT IS SPECIFIC

Why do you believe that God created you and what is His purpose for your life? Explain your list in detail:

_____

_____

_____

_____

_____

_____

_____

_____

_____

_____

_____

_____

_____

_____

_____

_____

_____

_____

_____

DESTINY GUIDE   MARCH

GOD KNOWS HOW TO PRODUCE POWER

Write a list of the gifts and/or talents God gave you that will influence and/or help other people in their lives.

_____

_____

_____

_____

_____

_____

_____

_____

_____

_____

_____

_____

_____

_____

_____

_____

_____

_____

Destiny Guide   April

God knows his purpose is painful but productive

Write a list of what you believe will come out of what you've experienced.

_____

_____

_____

_____

_____

_____

_____

_____

_____

_____

_____

_____

_____

_____

_____

_____

_____

DESTINY GUIDE   MAY

GOD HAS A DESIGNATED TIME TO WORK WITH YOU

List the things that have caused delays in your progress. What do you think you need to do to bring about resolution to these areas?

_____

_____

_____

_____

_____

_____

_____

_____

_____

_____

_____

_____

_____

_____

_____

_____

_____

DESTINY GUIDE   JUNE

GOD'S PLAN IS TO TAKE YOU ON A FAR JOURNEY TO SEE AND EXPERIENCE HIS GOODNESS

Write a list of things you'd like to experience in life that will only happen by the help of God.

_____

_____

_____

_____

_____

_____

_____

_____

_____

_____

_____

_____

_____

_____

_____

_____

_____

_____

DESTINY GUIDE   JULY

GOD NEVER INTENDED TO SATISFY YOU TEMPORARILY, HIS PLAN IS TO MAKE YOU LIE DOWN IN GREEN PASTURES

How would you like to live the rest of your life on earth? How would you define success?

_____

_____

_____

_____

_____

_____

_____

_____

_____

_____

_____

_____

_____

_____

_____

_____

_____

DESTINY GUIDE   AUGUST

GOD MOVES WHEN YOU MOVE AND GOD SPEAKS WHEN YOU SPEAK

Write a list of things that you can do to help resolve your situation(s) with God's help.

_____

_____

_____

_____

_____

_____

_____

_____

_____

_____

_____

_____

_____

_____

_____

_____

_____

DESTINY GUIDE   SEPTEMBER

GOD COMMANDS EZEKIEL TO PROPHESY TO WHAT'S LEFT!

List the talents, gifts, abilities, associations, level of or type of education, business experiences and/or connections you may have that can assist you in your recovery stage. The purpose of this is to show you that you yet have something left to work with. These are recovery tools.

_____

_____

_____

_____

_____

_____

_____

_____

_____

_____

_____

_____

_____

_____

DESTINY GUIDE   OCTOBER

EXPECT SIGNS OF RECOVERY

Write a list of changes that have taken place in your life since you began this journey of recovery.

_____

_____

_____

_____

_____

_____

_____

_____

_____

_____

_____

_____

_____

_____

_____

_____

_____

_____

DESTINY GUIDE   NOVEMBER

GOD WILL GET THE GLORY OUT OF THIS

How will God be glorified by your recovery? How will it bless others?

_____

_____

_____

_____

_____

_____

_____

_____

_____

_____

_____

_____

_____

_____

_____

_____

_____

_____

DESTINY GUIDE   DECEMBER

WHATEVER YOU DO, DON'T QUIT NOW, IT'S NOT TOO LATE

What things are trying to hold you back that you need to say, *"DON'T TELL ME IT'S TOO LATE"* to?

_____

_____

_____

_____

_____

_____

_____

_____

_____

_____

_____

_____

_____

_____

_____

_____

_____